Englische Wirtschaftstexte für Ausbildung und Beruf

Englische Wirtschaftstexte für Ausbildung und Beruf

mit Erläuterungen und Übersetzungen

Herausgeberinnen:
Prof. Karin Hildebrandt und Prof. Eva Knudsen

Betriebswirtschaftlicher Verlag Dr. Th. Gabler · Wiesbaden

ISBN 3 409 800115

Copyright by Dr. Gabler-Verlag · Wiesbaden 1975

Vorwort

ENGLISCHE WIRTSCHAFTSTEXTE FÜR AUSBILDUNG UND BERUF wendet sich in erster Linie an Studierende und Lernende im wirtschaftswissenschaftlichen Bereich und ist für Schule und Erwachsenenbildung bestimmt. Es bietet Arbeits- und Diskussionsstoff im Unterricht an Fachoberschulen, Wirtschaftsgymnasien und in der Fremdsprachenbildung im wirtschaftswissenschaftlichen Bereich an Fachhochschule und Universität.

ENGLISCHE WIRTSCHAFTSTEXTE FÜR AUSBILDUNG UND BERUF gibt dem Studierenden Mittel an die Hand, seine sprachlichen Grundkenntnisse weiterzuentwickeln und sich sprachlich auf für ihn beruflich wichtigen Gebieten zu spezialisieren. Es dient als Vorbereitung und Übung für das Verstehen von Fachliteratur und kann insbesondere immer dann eingesetzt werden, wenn der Studierende in die Lage versetzt werden soll, Gespräche über wirtschafts-, währungs- und sozialpolitische Themen auf englisch zu führen.

ENGLISCHE WIRTSCHAFTSTEXTE FÜR AUSBILDUNG UND BERUF enthält englische und amerikanische Originaltexte, die so ausgewählt und bearbeitet wurden, daß mehrere sprachliche Niveaustufen angesprochen werden, d. h. der Studierende mit englischen Grundkenntnissen findet ebenso geeignetes Arbeits- und Übungsmaterial wie der sprachlich weiter Fortgeschrittene. Er wird vom passiven Lesen zu aktiver Bearbeitung des Textmaterials geführt.

Die Vokabelliste (Vocabulary) im Anschluß an jeden Text soll dem Lernenden helfen, die Texte leichter zu verstehen und sich sofort den unmittelbaren Problemen zuzuwenden. Gleichzeitig wird ihm durch die meist auf englisch in leicht verständlicher Form gegebene Bedeutung der Wörter — nur in Ausnahmefällen wurde wegen der Eindeutigkeit davon Abstand genommen — die Möglichkeit gegeben, ohne allzu großen Aufwand seinen Wortschatz zu erweitern.

Die Fragen zum Text (Questions on the text) bilden den für das Selbststudium wichtigsten Bestandteil des einzelnen Textkapitels. Hier muß bewiesen werden, ob der Text wirklich verstanden wurde, da sich die Fragen nur durch richtiges Leseverstehen beantworten lassen. Um die Beantwortung zu erleichtern, wurden die Fragen chronologisch angeordnet.

Die Diskussionspunkte (Points for discussion) sollen Anregung geben, sich mit den im Zusammenhang mit dem Text stehenden Problemen zu befassen. Sie eignen sich besonders als Diskussionsgrundlage für Arbeitsgemeinschaften, in denen in Kleingruppen (ca. 6 Teilnehmer) das aktive Sprechen in der englischen Sprache geübt werden soll. Zur Vorbereitung der Diskussion könnte ein Teilnehmer zu dem gewählten Thema kurz auf englisch referieren. Es empfiehlt sich, aus der Gruppe einen Diskussionsleiter zu wählen, der dafür sorgt, daß gegensätzliche Meinungen herausgearbeitet werden, und der von Zeit zu Zeit kurze Zusammenfassungen der diskutierten Probleme gibt. Außerdem können die Diskussionspunkte auch als Themen für essay-writing benutzt werden.

Zu jedem Text findet sich im Anhang eine Übersetzung. Wir sind uns der Problematik einer Übersetzung voll bewußt und möchten deshalb ganz besonders darauf hinweisen, daß diese Übersetzungsmuster keinesfalls eine alleingültige Version darstellen. Wir haben uns dennoch dazu entschlossen, um dem autodidaktisch Lernenden eine Kontrollmöglichkeit zu geben. Er kann seine Antworten auf die Fragen zum Leseverstehen überprüfen und, falls er zweisprachig arbeiten möchte, seine Übersetzung mit dem Übersetzungsmuster vergleichen.

ENGLISCHE WIRTSCHAFTSTEXTE FÜR AUSBILDUNG UND BERUF dient der Schulung des Leseverstehens und aktiven Sprechens, zweier Fertigkeiten also, die im beruflichen Bereich besonders wichtig sind.

Karin Hildebrandt   Eva Knudsen

Inhaltsverzeichnis

	Seite
Consumer Income and Spending	9
The POOR Getting poorer and poorer	13
Growth Potential of the U.S. Economy	20
Workers in the Boardrooms	24
See How They Grow	28
The Example of Shell International	31
On with Exxon	35
Facing the economic facts of life	37
How to Fight Inflation	41
Bonn hopes to deflate the boom	46
A Secret IMF Proposal for Monetary Reform Urges Radical Changes	48
What Marshall Aid did for Europe	54
The year of the Grand Disillusion	59
More cultural contacts in Europe	64
European Road Construction	67
Common transport policy	71
Trouble again with monster lorries	74
Clean-Air Buff	77
A fresh breeze from Stockholm	79
Spaceship earth or mucky rivers?	83
Take a sober look at doomsday	87
World food situation worst for years	90
Two significant post-war years	93
Agreement on Enough (arms control)	97

Consumer Income and Spending

Rising population in conjunction with rising incomes will add up to a sizable growth in consumer demand over the next two decades. In that interval, real personal consumption expenditures will, like GNP, substantially more than double. Since the economy will be growing at a considerably faster pace than the population, there will also be a steady escalation in real per capita consumption. Currently, each American spends, on average, about $3,300 annually, but by 1990 this figure will be close to $6,000, in terms of today's dollars. This anticipated improvement in living standards will be faster than experienced in the prior two decades, principally because, in the coming period, a larger proportion of the population will be of working age.

We are, in fact, experiencing a significant reshuffle in the distribution of income in real terms; each year, many millions of families move upward in the earning scale. In the past, this process consisted mainly of a shift from adequate to comfortable levels of income. In the coming decades, however, a large proportion of American families will have the means to purchase the products and services generally associated with an abundant life. Currently, about 12 million, or less than one fourth, of all families have annual earnings exceeding $15,000, but 20 years from now such families will be a substantial majority. By 1990, families with incomes exceeding $15,000 (in 1971 dollars) will number well over 40 million and account for close to 60% of all families. About one out of every four families in 1990 will have an income of over $25,000 a year, compared with one out of twenty today.

This upward progression will not, however, entirely eliminate poverty. Although poverty will be less widespread, its persistence will represent an even greater social issue, precisely because of the economy's increased capacity to alleviate it. For example, 4½ million families today have annual incomes less than $3,000; there will still be about 2½ million families with incomes below $3,000 (in 1971 dollars) in 1990. This, however, is entirely a statistical projection, which does not take into account social programs which might be initiated in the coming years.

As a family moves up in the earning scale, each dollar of additional income is spent differently—relatively less goes for necessities, more becomes available for other things. For example, consumer outlays for food and for footwear increased by about 2½ % a year, on average, between 1955 and 1970, whereas consumer spending for foreign travel and for higher education grew more than 6 %, on average. In the future as in the past, some sectors of the consumer market will grow much more rapidly than others. The response of consumers to rising spending power in the recent past provides at least a rough indication of what might be anticipated for the era ahead.

Übersetzung auf Seite 102

Vocabulary

abundant	here: luxurious
account for v.	here: represent
alleviate v. (ə'liːvieɪt)	eliminate, relieve
annually	yearly, a year
anticipated	expected
associated with	connected with
(in) conjunction with	together with
currently	at present, now, today
eliminate v.	do away with, abolish, put an end to
exceed v.	be higher than, surpass, go beyond
GNP (gross national product) (grəus)	Bruttosozialprodukt
indication n.	sign, hint
issue n.	problem
means (pl.) n.	here: money
outlays (pl.) n.	expenditure
per capita	per person, per head
persistence n.	steadfast continuance
prior	here: past

projection n.   estimate, forecast
reshuffle n.   re-grouping
response n.   reaction
shift n.   move
sizable   substantial, considerable

Questions on the text

1. How, according to the authors, will real personal consumption expenditure develop over the next two decades?
2. What will lead to an increase in real per capita consumption?
3. How do the authors see the difference in the redistribution of income in real terms between the past and the future?
4. What proportion of all American families earn more than $15,000 a year at present?
5. What do the authors say about the development of poverty within the next twenty years?
6. How are increasing incomes expected to be spent?
7. On what do the authors base their projection for the time until 1990?

Points for discussion

1. With rising incomes more and more people think of building their own houses. Discuss the advantages and disadvantages of private housing.
2. With rising incomes the number of cars per family will also rise. How is this related to
   a) government expenditure,
   b) pollution,
   c) energy problems?
3. By 1990 foreign travel will rise by over 6 per cent annually. State your opinion on the benefits and drawbacks of an increase in tourism.
4. Discuss society's problems of an overproportional rise in higher education.

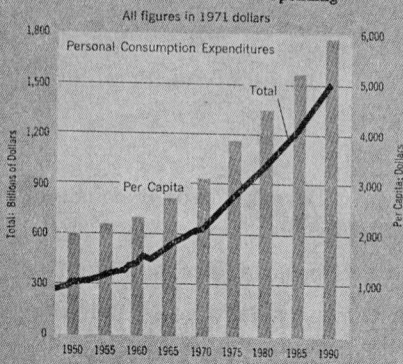

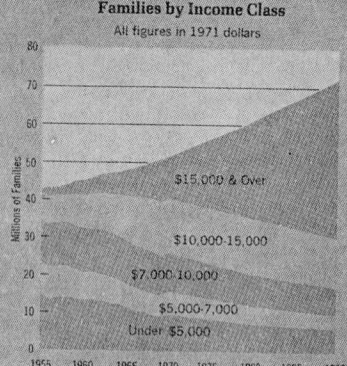

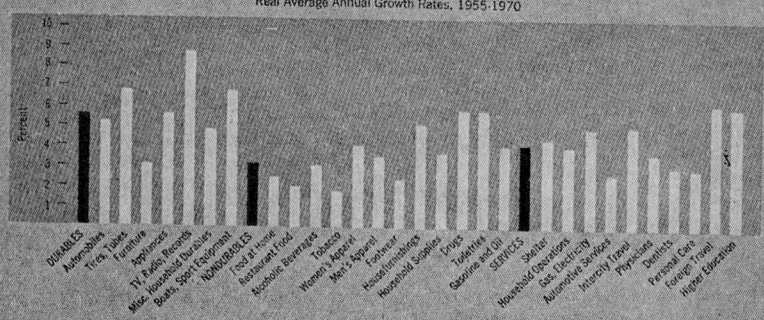

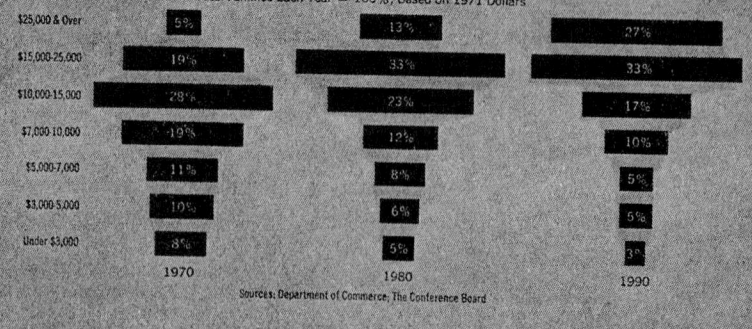

THE POOR
Getting poorer and poorer...

ON THE VERY last day of the exploratory talks before Stage Three between the Government and the TUC, new evidence was published showing the extent to which the well-off have been getting better off (after tax) and the poor becoming worse off, since the Conservatives came into office. These figures, which can be deduced from the Familiy Expenditure Survey for 1972, still remain to be absorbed by the policy-makers. It could bring new policy directions which could provide the basis for a future incomes policy, whether under this Government or some future one.

THE FES provides the most up-to-date details of the distribution of income and the first available information for 1972. It therefore offers for the first time an opportunity to assess the Conservative Government's impact, at least in the short run, on the post-tax spread of wages and salaries. Its moral for current economic policy, though so far ignored, is immense.

By re-working the data given for the gross and net spread of income, it is possible to link it with similar information in the latest Inland Revenue Statistics, relating to 1970, in order to obtain direct comparisons with the official statisticians' tables of income distribution up to 1967 (after which these tables unfortunately ceased to be published). The results, assembled here, tell a story far removed from the popular myth, promulgated by many Conservatives, of a flattening juggernaut of equality.

What has really happened over the last quarter century is that the richest tenth in the population have seen their share of income fall, in uneven steps, from slightly over two and a half times their proportionate share of total national income to slightly under two and a half times. The middle mass who form three-fifths of the population have steadily increased their income, sometimes quite fast and sometimes only marginally, from slightly less than the share of national income proportionate to their numbers to somewhat more. The poorest third of the population, however, after starting with a share of national income which was less than half that proportionate to their numbers, have found their position tending to deteriorate.

In suggesting above that the figures in the table show the extent to which post-tax incomes have been redistributed under the present Government, I err on the conservative side. In fact, the figures for the period 1970—1972 understate the true picture. For one thing, they take no account of the increased charges for school meals, prescriptions and other medical accessories, and council housing (which are of course paid for out of after-tax income). And at the top end of the scale, the increase in the share of after-tax income of the richest 10 % between 1970 and 1972 has been greater than that shown in the table.

Shares of total national post-tax income secured by the rich, the middle mass and the poor.

Groups of income recipients	Share of total national post-tax income at:					
	1949 (%)	1957 (%)	1963 (%)	1967 (%)	1970 (%)	1972 (%)
the richest 10 %	27.1	24.0	25.2	24.3	21.5	22.0
the middle 60 %	58.3	62.5	63.0	63.7	63.8	65.5
the poorest 30 %	14.6	13.4	11.8	12.0	14.7	12.5

In other words, the figure 22.0 % in the final column is an understatement. This is partly because response rates to the FES are lower among the well-off, partly because people under-state their investment incomes to a greater extent to the FES than they do in their tax-returns, and partly (to a very minor extent) due to a technical reason arising from my adjustment of the data. The upshot is, the richest 10 % of the income-earning population have enjoyed a significant increase in their share of total after-tax income. Contrary to the generally received wisdom, the ideology and politics of the Government in power have had a major impact in channelling income between the better off and the poorer.

The middle income groups gained in their share of after-tax income too—in other words, both the upper and the middle groups gained at the expense of the poorest 30 %. This impression could however be exaggerated by the figures for 1970—1972, as the 14.7 % share of income for the poorest 30 % given for 1970 may be slightly overstated, due to the cut-off figure of £275 a year below which the Inland Revenue does not record people as income-earners.

Even allowing for this, the trend is both clear and politically consistent. The richest 10 % found their position eroded throughout most of the post-war period, enjoying however a temporary increase in their share in the early 1960s, when the Macmillan government was in office.

The trend of a diminishing share for this group was resumed under the Wilson government, but was reversed again after 1970 (to a greater extent than the figures show) under the present government. And as for the poor, it is clear that (despite the qualifications one must enter about the figures) their share has varied, broadly speaking, inversely with that of the rich.

The reason for the latest changes shown in the table was the enormous reduction in taxes in the 1971—72 budgets, which was heavily concentrated on the richest tenth in the population, and prevented their decline in pre-tax income being translated into a fall in post-tax receipts. For during 1970—72 the pre-tax income of the richest tenth actually fell, yet their post-tax income rose by at least ½ %.

Against this background, Heath's strongest card for an incomes deal is that the share of the poor is declining and must be reversed. One way of achieving this would be to relax some of the grosser inequities of the jungle of tax reliefs and allowances that have grown up higgledy-piggledy over time, and to use the proceeds for a major boost to pensions and benefits for the dependent groups and for raising the tax threshold for the lower-paid.

The effect of granting large-scale tax reliefs, whose value rose directly with income, is of course to negate the progressivity of our so-called "penal" income tax structure in the higher reaches and is the main reason, in conjunction with the maintenance of percentage differentials in gross pay, for the remarkable resilience of income inequality in our society. For both the marginal rate of tax on earned income (top rate 75 % at £20,000 per year) and the effective tax rate over the whole span of income (less than 50 % at £20,000) are substantially reduced by an array of reliefs.

These tax reliefs were worth to their recipients in 1972, according to the latest Government figures, a total of some £2,500 m—heavily (though not wholly) concentrated on the top 10 %. This was made up as follows: relief on employees' contributions (£170 m) and employers' contributions (£650 m) to occupational pension schemes, on life assurance contributions (£315 m), on mortgage interest payments (£390 m), on bank loan interest (£7 m), and as child tax allowances (£930 m). Altogether these tax reliefs and allowances equalled no less than 37 % of the total yield of income tax plus surtax in 1972.

Their effect in eroding the supposedly progressive nature of income tax, and inhibiting fiscal redistribution, can be seen clearly from the evidence of Inland Revenue Statistics 1971 (Table 105). This shows that the life assurance tax reliefs, for example, were worth no less than 23 times more per recipient to those with incomes over £10,000 per year than to those with incomes below £1,000 per year.

If these tax reliefs were tapered down in the upper income brackets so as to reduce their overall cost to the Exchequer by about a third, it would release sufficient extra resources both to add £2 per week to the retirement pension as well as increasing family allowances by 50 p per week, of particular value to low-paid workers.

Such a solution could offer greater fairness in taxation and income distribution "at a stroke." There is little point in having an income tax structure which is meant to be progressive, yet which includes a number of tax reliefs the effect of which is highly regressive.

Übersetzung auf Seite 104

Vocabulary

adjustment n.	hier: Aufbereitung (von Daten)
allowance n.	hier: Vergünstigungen
array n.	hier: Ausnutzung, Anwendung
assemble v.	gather together, collect
assess v.	estimate
cease v.	stop, discontinue
consistent	unvarying
council housing	sozialer Wohnungsbau
current	present
cut-off figure	here: exclusion
deal n.	bargaining
deduce v.	extract
deteriorate v.	get worse
differential n.	difference
erode v.	wear away
evidence n.	proof
exaggerate v.	deliberately make more of
exploratory (eks'plɔːrətərı)	investigatory, examining
gross (grəvs)	before any deductions
grosser	greater
higgledy-piggledy	haphazardly; zufällig
ignore v.	overlook deliberately
impact n.	effect, influence
inequity n.	inequality
inhibit v.	hinder, hamper
inversely	in an opposite direction
juggernaut n.	giant
marginally	slightly
moral n.	lesson to be learned
mortgage n. ('mɔːgɪdʒ)	Hypothek
negate v.	invalidate
overstate v.	deliberately make more of
penal ('piːnl)	Straf-
prescription n.	Arztrezept
proceeds (pl.) n.	money received
promulgate v.	put about
resilience n. (rɪ'zɪlıəns)	ability to resist
response n.	answer, reply

17

2 Hildebrandt / Knudsen

resume v. (rɪ'zju:m)	take up again
re-work v.	here: process, adapt, adjust
stroke n.	Streich
surtax n.	Sondersteuer für hohe Einkommen, Ergänzungsabgabe
taper down v.	here: reduce
tax-return n.	Steuererklärung
threshold n.	lower limit, base limit
TUC (Trades Union Congress)	Dachverband der britischen Gewerkschaften
understate v.	underrate
upshot n.	outcome
yield n.	here: amount, receipts

Questions on the text

1. What does the author say about the income development of the well-off and the poor since the Conservatives came into office?
2. What information does the FES provide?
3. What has happened to the income of the middle class over the last 25 years?
4. What has happened to the share of income of the richest 10 %?
5. How has the share of income of the poorest third of the population developed?
6. Why are the figures for the period between 1970 and 1972 incorrect?
7. Why is the figure 22.0 % in the final column an understatement?
8. At whose expense did the upper and the middle income groups gain?
9. Why can it be assumed that the income figure for the poorest 30 % given for 1970 may be slightly overstated?
10. What effect had the Macmillan Government on the incomes development of the richest 10 %?
11. How are the income shares of the rich and of the poor related?
12. How did the tax reduction in the 1971—72 budgets affect the richest 10 % of the population?

13. What way of improving the situation of the poor is described by the author?
14. What reasons are mentioned for the income inequality?
15. How were the total tax reliefs of £2,500 m. in 1972 made up?
16. Why are the tax reliefs of higher value to the rich than to the poor?
17. What solution, according to the author, could offer greater fairness in taxation and income distribution?

Points for discussion

1. Compare the tax system, as far as it is described in the text, with the situation in your own country.
2. Discuss methods of the government to influence the distribution of incomes.
3. Name and discuss the governments' sources of income.
4. Where does the government's money go? State whether, in your opinion, government activity in all these fields is justified.
5. If you were finance minister, how would you try to reach fairness in taxation and income distribution?

Growth Potential of the U.S. Economy

The total output of the U.S. economy in dollars of constant purchasing power has more than doubled in the last 20 years. Goods and services are now being produced at an annual rate of more than $1 trillion. Under conditions of full employment of capital and labor, the gross national product of the nation in 1971 prices is projected to reach a total of more than $2.4 trillion by 1990.

Owing to variations in the level of activity as a result of the business cycle, war, and inflation, the growth rate of GNP has fluctuated widely from year to year. The pace of economic growth has also varied considerably over periods of similar cyclical activity. Measured from peak to peak of the business cycle, the growth rate was more than twice as great from 1948 to 1953 as it was from 1957 to 1960, for example.

In preparing our projections, we assume that the economy will experience cyclical variation during the next 20 years; however, the growth paths shown are those that represent the long-term trend, rather than forecasts of individual years. For the entire period from 1948 to 1969, the rate of growth of real output averaged 3.9%. This rate is expected to accelerate to 4.2% for the period from 1969 to 1990 largely as a result of a more rapid rate of growth of employment anticipated in the next two decades than in the previous two.

The main source of growth in the next 20 years will be the rise in GNP per worker, which is expected to go from $12,500 in 1970 to $22,500 in 1990, in 1971 prices. This was also the principal source of the doubling of gross national product in the preceding two decades. One of the conventions in measuring the gross national product is that the general government sector, unlike government enterprises, has no change in productivity. Both the historical and the projected gains in GNP per worker, therefore, stem entirely from the private sector.

The composition of expenditures for the gross national product is not anticipated to show substantial changes on a long-term basis over the next 20 years. Cyclical variation produces wide short-term swings in composition, affecting primarily investment expenditures and consumption of durable goods. Considerable variation also results from activities of government, particularly in periods of war.

Over the long term, we project that consumption expenditures will account for about 60 % of the gross national product in 1990, approximately the same proportion as held in the last two decades, aside from the irregular fluctuations just discussed. By 1990, therefore, consumption expenditures should exceed $1.5 trillion in terms of 1971 price levels, a rise of 135 % in consumer purchases of goods and services from the present. The importance of government expenditures is expected to remain stable, at about 24 % of GNP, yielding a dollar total of $570 billion in 1990.

Investment expenditures, at 15 % of GNP through the 1960's, are expected to decline slightly in relative importance in the two following decades. The dollar amounts is projected at $330 billion in 1990. Net exports of goods and services, a relatively minor component of GNP, are expected to rise in the first decade, and then to level off, in absolute terms after 1980.

Übersetzung auf Seite 109

Vocabulary

anticipate v.	expect
assume v.	understand, suppose
business cycle	Konjunktur
entirely	completely, exclusively
exceed v.	be greater than, surpass
expenditure n.	money spent
gains (pl.) n.	here: increase
general government sector	hier: Bereich der öffentl. Hand
government enterprise	hier: öffentliche Unternehmungen
gross national product (GNP abbr.)	Bruttosozialprodukt

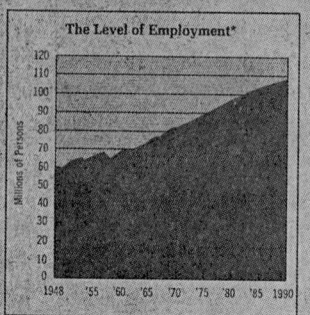

*Includes Military

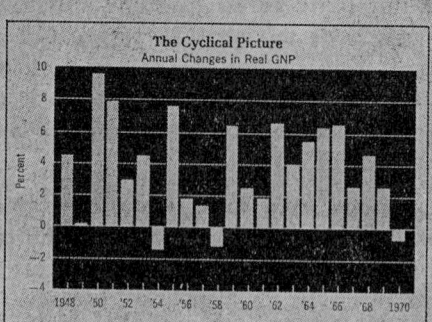

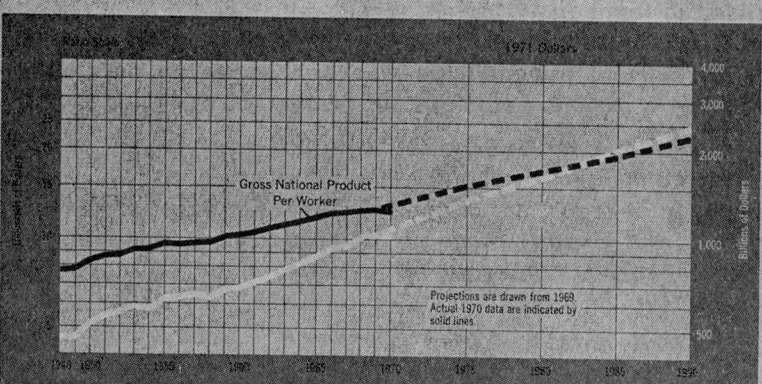

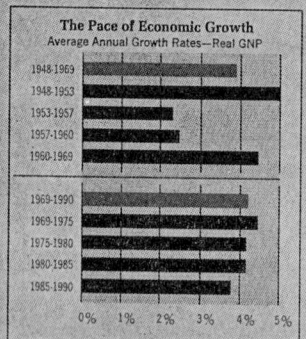

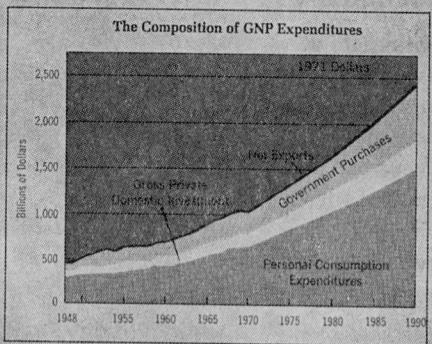

Sources: Department of Labor; Department of Commerce; The Conference Board

gross national product per worker	Bruttosozialprodukt pro Kopf der Beschäftigten
growth rate (rate of growth)	Wachstumsrate
pace n.	speed
peak n.	highest point
purchasing power	Kaufkraft
output n.	Leistungskraft, Ertrag
yield v.	produce, give

Questions on the text

1. What can you say about the American economy in the past twenty years?
2. Under what conditions can the GNP rise up to $2.4 trillion in 1990?
3. Why has the growth rate of GNP fluctuated yearly?
4. Will the growth rate of real output rise? If so, why?
5. What was the main reason for the doubling of GNP in the last twenty years?
6. How important are government expenditures for the GNP?
7. Is the growth projected in real or nominal terms?

Points for discussion

1. What do you think about the forecasts that are made in the text?
2. What can you say about the relation between income and consumption expenditure?
3. Make a comparison of the importance of the private sector and the government sector for GNP.
4. Which factors contributing decisively to the welfare of the individual are not considered in the projections?
5. The U.S. gross national product is projected to rise by 140 % by 1990. What factors could prevent the individual income from rising in relation to the GNP?

Workers in the boardrooms

Mr. Wilson wants to involve the individual, as a free citizen, in the managerial and industrial decisions that affect him. Yet many trade unionists believe that works councils are a farce, that employee share-holding is a sop, and that worker-directors are nothing but a confidence trick. Who is right? Mr. Wilson has been making workers' participation an important theme in his "Edinburgh series" of speeches. At Blackpool he set out a number of specific measures—joint decision making on factory planning and production techniques; compulsory works councils; a two-tier top management structure, with workers on supervisory boards; better trade union services, and others. It is a remarkable array. But will it convert his own ranks—and, no less, the entrenched conservatism of boardrooms?

He has important allies. The bureaucrats in Brussels, perhaps surprisingly, are among them. Most European countries are well ahead of Britain in providing for "employee participation." The new draft EEC company law has the two-tier structure which Mr. Wilson now wants, together with mandatory requirements on works councils. And countries such as West Germany and the Netherlands have had years of experience in working this system, though with somewhat mixed results. It is worth trying here, though it will not remove all friction and frustration.

Mr. Wilson unintentionally demonstrated the limitations of what worker participation can achieve. In one of his broadcasts, having justly blasted the inhumanity of asset-strippers who acquire a factory to close it down, he referred feelingly to the steelworkers of Ebbw Vale whom he had seen during their demonstration in London. These steelworkers, however, came from the British industry that has the most advanced forms of participation— established by Mr. Wilson himself. Under the 1967 Act the British Steel Corporation appoints employee directors to divisional boards. The experiment is said on the whole to have been a success. But no amount of worker participation can save a factory, steelworks or shipyard which has become obsolescent. The steel industry has seen vast changes of technology in recent years. The decision to develop a 12-million-ton integrated works on Teesside as the next stage after Scunthorpe seems technically correct. The impending rundown at Ebbw Vale and Shotton is an unavoidable consequence. If British steel is to remain competitive it must modernise. As in steel, so in other industries: no degree of worker involvement can avert the need for such decisions unless all British industry is to ossify.

Thinking is taking place also on the Conservative side. A useful study has been published by the Conservative Political Centre— Bryan Cassidy's "Workers on the Board," price 15p. This looks with interest on the two-tier structure but stops short of recommending it. It simply expects more companies to experiment on BSC lines. It endorses statutory works councils. It rightly says that there is too much secrecy in boardrooms and among managements.

Two acute difficulties impede progress. Directors must be able to discuss future planning and future contracts confidentially and dispassionately. Will the workers let their representatives do so, without demanding that they report back at every stage? And, ultimately, there has to be a division of profits between workers, shareholders, and reserves. Can it be achieved without a bloody battle? Mr. Wilson, the CPC, and many others are sensible in looking for new ways.

Übersetzung auf Seite 111

Vocabulary

achieve v.	get
array (ə'reɪ)	display
avert v.	prevent, avoid
blast v.	hier: verdammen
board n.	group of persons controlling a business or business department
boardroom n.	place in which meetings (of the Board of Directors) are held
compulsory (kəm'pʌlsərɪ)	obligatory
confidence trick n.	Bauernfängerei

CPC	Conservative Political Centre
draft n.	hier: Entwurf
employee n.	Arbeitnehmer (opposite: employer)
endorse v.	support, approve
entrenched	firmly established
friction n.	difference of opinion leading to quarrel
impede v. (ımpi:d)	hinder
impending	imminent, threatening
joint	common
mandatory	compulsory, obligatory
obsolescent	becoming out of date
ossify v.	becoming rigid, unprogressive
remove v. (rı'mu:v)	abolish
rundown n.	reduction and eventual abolition of sth. that is no longer considered to be useful
sensible	wise
sop n.	etwa: Beruhigungspille, Beschwichtigungsmittel
stop short of	not go as far as
supervisory board	etwa: Aufsichtsrat einer AG in Deutschland
trade unionist (member of a trade union)	Gewerkschaftler
two-tier structure	zweistufige Struktur, Dualstruktur
unavoidable	inevitable

Questions on the text

1 What were Mr. Wilson's proposals for introducing employee participation?

2. Why do many trade unionists disagree with Mr. Wilson over the questions of worker participation?

3. Has the experience of other West European countries been positive?

4. Can you describe what the word "assetstripper" means in this text?
5. Which branch of industry in Britain has the most advanced forms of worker participation?
6. Which form of worker participation does the CPC-study support?
7. Where does the writer of the article see the main difficulties preventing progress?

Points for discussion

1. Do you think that worker participation in managerial and industrial decisions is a legitimate claim? If so, why?
2. Through employee participation the trade unions only want to strengthen their own powerful position. Discuss this statement.
3. Where do you see the differences of opinion between the Conservative Party and the Labour Party in the question of employee participation?
4. In your opinion, how could the profits of a company be justly divided among workers, shareholders and reserves?

See How They Grow

FORTUNE'S annual compilation of figures for the nation's 500 largest industrial companies, published this week, serves as a kind of X-ray of the corporate sector of the U.S. economy: it illuminates trends that can be discerned only dimly in individual company reports. Among last year's notable tendencies were a somewhat disconcerting ability of the big companies to cut employment while increasing sales, a continued sharp decline in merger activity and what looks like the beginning of a turn away from diversification.

Overall, 1971 was a middling-good year for the 500. They increased total sales 8.4%, to nearly $503 billion, and profits 8%, to $23.4 billion. The figures, however, are considerably distorted by the standout performance of General Motors, which benefited from a banner year for auto sales. By itself, G.M. accounted for three-quarters of the profit gain posted by the entire group. Other giants got bigger, too. Seven companies joined the once-exclusive billion-dollar-sales club, raising membership to 127. The newcomers: Philip Morris, Nabisco, Bristol-Myers, Combustion Engineering, Campbell Soup, Iowa Beef Processors and CBS. Meanwhile, Standard Oil of California became the twelfth U.S. company to register sales of more than $5 billion a year.

The 500 also slightly increased their leverage in the U.S. economy —though in such a way as to raise questions about their efficiency. Last year they accounted for 66% of all sales by industrial companies, up from 65% in 1970 and little more than 50% a decade earlier. Their share of industrial profits, however, stayed put at 75%, almost unchanged from 1970. Obviously, smaller companies have been increasing their profitability more rapidly than the large corporations, suggesting perhaps that some of the 500—G.M. excluded—have pushed past their optimum size.

In one respect, the 500 demonstrated a pointed kind of efficiency: they sliced employment by 2%, to 14.3 million, while increasing sales. As a result, their average sales per employee rose 10%, to

$35.166. G.M., Ford and ITT, the three biggest employers., all added to their payrolls. But General Electric, the fourth largest, chopped its work force 8.5 %, letting 33,600 people go.

Other highlights:
▶ Only two mergers occurred among the 500 last year: National Steel acquired Granite City Steel, and General Host took over Cudahy. That was the smallest number since 1958; it compared with a recent peak of 23 in 1968. Apparently, the Justice Department's opposition to big mergers is helping to hold them down.

▶ Twenty-four companies wrote off a startling total of $1.5 billion in various losses last year, and some of the largest represented the cost of unwinding profitless diversification. RCA wrote off $490 million as the expected loss on liquidation of its computer business. American-Standard has shucked its mining-equipment and air-conditioning divisions, and is getting out of recreational-land development, mobile-home parks and foreign housing. Write-off: $122 million.

Übersetzung auf Seite 113

Vocabulary

banner year	Rekordjahr
chop v.	cut
dimly	vaguely
discern v.	here: see, make out
disconcerting	upsetting
distort v.	twist out of shape
compilation n.	Zusammenstellung, Aufstellung
leverage n. ('li:vərɪdʒ)	powerful position
merger n.	combining of business companies, fusing
middling	mean, average
payroll n.	here: number of employees
profit gain	Gewinnzuwachs
shuck v.	abstreifen, ablegen
startling	surprising, shocking
unwind v.	abwickeln
work force	labour force
X-ray	Röntgenaufnahme

Questions on the text

1. Why is the mentioned compilation considered as a kind of X-ray of the American economy?
2. What was the most outstanding feature in the big companies' actions last year?
3. Why do the sales figures mentioned for 1971 not provide a genuine picture of what actually happened?
4. What is meant by the "billion-dollar sales club"? When are you allowed to join it?
5. How did the 500 give proof of their efficiency?
6. What reason can you find in the text for the decreasing merger activity in American industry?
7. Can you give three examples of industrial branches which liquidated last year?

Points for discussion

1. Concentration is very often motivated by rising research and development costs. Cite some examples of whether this could be true and give specific reasons.
2. Try to find reasons for the apparent greater profitability of big companies in contrast to small companies.
3. Do you think that the trend towards fewer and bigger companies influences the innovative ability of industry?
4. Do you think growing concentration affects high marketing flexibility?
5. Comment on shifting consumer demand patterns.

The example of Shell International

Concern about the growth of multinational companies and their possible threat to the host government's authority has spread from the developing to the industrialised countries in the last few years. The debate has been mostly focused on the power these companies wield and the need for governments to devise ways in which the companies can be made accountable.

It is not often that the companies themselves make a contribution to the debate. Nor has much been said before about relations between host governments and foreign companies when the local operations of a multinational run into serious difficulty and the scale of its activities has to be reduced. This may not have happened very often, but the practical problems encountered in one specific instance are described by Mr. Geoffrey Chandler, a Shell International director, in the current Moorgate and Wall Street review. Although the events took place in Trinidad, during the time Mr. Chandler was Shell chief executive there, the lessons are applicable to situations much nearer home.

Trinidad was one of the world's first oil producers. But prolific oil finds elsewhere and the trend towards siting refineries in the main oil-consuming markets had made the island's oil fields and refineries grossly uncompetitive by the early 1960s. To stave off retrenchment, Shell tried to develop new techniques of extracting crude oil from the island's low-grade reserves. The new methods proved technically feasible, but they offered no prospect of becoming economic. The only alternative, therefore, was to cut manpower by half—a prospect which, with 15 per cent unemployment on the island and double as much among school-leavers, neither the host Government nor the powerful local trade union were likely to accept very readily.

Guided by recommendations of the International Labour Organisation, the Company adopted what ought to be the classic management approach to redundancy. Some of the measures Mr. Chandler describes are appropriate only in a developing country

—the repatriation of expatriates, assisted passages for those employers who wished to return to other Caribbean islands, and the sale at low prices of equipment used in ancillary services, like printing, cleaning, and house maintenance, to employees who wanted to establish their own businesses.

Whether a company should provide or support retraining facilities and help employees to find other jobs must obviously depend upon local circumstances. But several other steps described by Mr. Chandler could with advantage be included in any retrenchment programme. Besides providing clear and full information at all levels, it is also important to ensure that managers and supervisors are convinced of the necessity and fairness of what is proposed otherwise it may not be possible to count on their co-operation. At the same time, there should be economies at the top as well as at the bottom. And, because the provision of lump sum benefits in addition to normal accumulated benefits in order to encourage voluntary retirement can lead to an unbalanced age structure, it may also be desirable to reduce the minimum pensionable age without reducing pension benefits.

Because the company in this particular situation showed a sense of fairness and a sensitivity to the human aspects, it won the consent of its employees, the local trade union, and the host Government and thereby succeeded in its main aim. The difficulties faced by a multinational company differ only in scale from those of a national company. But perhaps the underlying moral of this and other examples of massive retrenchment, as Mr. Chandler himself remarks, is that companies should react to economic, technological, or competitive change as it occurs rather than to wait until major surgery becomes unavoidable.

Übersetzung auf Seite 115

Vocabulary

age structure	Alterspyramide
ancillary (æn'sɪlərɪ)	subordinate
applicable to	transferable to, relevant to
classic management approach	klassische Verhaltensweise der Arbeitgeber

crude	raw, in a natural state
devise v.	find
economies (pl.) n.	Einsparungen
encountered in one specific instance	in einem spezifischen Fall aufgetreten
feasible ('fi:səbl)	practicable
finds (pl.) n.	findings
focus v.	concentrate
host n. (həust)	person who entertains guests
host government	Regierung des Gastlandes
lump sum	one payment for a number of separate sums
make sb. accountable	make sb. accept the responsibility
manpower n.	labour force
prolific	rich, immense
prospect n.	Aussicht, Möglichkeit
redundancy n.	here: too many workers and not enough work
repatriation of expatriates	Rückführung ausländischer Staatsbürger
retraining facilities	Umschulungsmöglichkeiten
retrenchment n.	Einschränkung, Verkleinerung, Einsparung
site v.	establish, build
stave off v.	keep off, delay
supervisor n.	hier: Werkmeister
surgery n. ('sə:dʒəri)	treating diseases by operation
voluntary retirement	freiwillige Pensionierung
wield v.	have and exercise

Questions on the text

1. What is the potential danger for host governments when they have powerful multinational companies in their countries?
2. Which example does Mr. G. Chandler refer to?
3. What had contributed towards making Trinidad's oil refineries uncompetitive?

4. What did the Shell company do to remedy the situation?
5. Why did this attempt fail?
6. Which other alternative was taken into account?
7. Why did the trade unions object to this plan?
8. Can you describe some measures applicable only in developing countries?
9. Which reasons are mentioned that could lead to an imbalance of the age structure in a company?
10. How did Shell succeed in solving the problem in the end?

Points for discussion
1. Try to analyse the differences in the difficulties faced by multinational and national companies.
2. State the causes of the immense growth of multinational companies.
3. Discuss how a reduction of the minimum pensionable age helps to curb unemployment.
4. Do you think that employees at all levels should be provided with clear and full information on management decisions? (Give reasons for your answer)
5. Will, in your opinion, the influence of the trade unions be increased or decreased by the growth of multinational companies?

On with EXXON

Along with Coke, Jeep, Mace, Band-Aid and Levi's, one of the world's most famous trademarks is Esso. It is used by Standard Oil Co. (New Jersey) in foreign countries and many parts of the U.S., where Esso is the trademark of the domestic operating arm, Humble Oil and Refining Co. Trouble is, legal restrictions following the 1911 breakup of the old Standard Oil trust have barred Humble from brandishing the Esso name in 20 states. In parts of the South and West, the company uses the label Enco, or, in Ohio, Humble.

After decades of grappling with the national advertising and marketing problems that a multiplicity of trademarks entails, Humble officers last week announced final agreement on a compromise. As of next January, the firm will change its name to Exxon Co., and in July its three gasolines will become Exxon, Exxon Plus and Exxon Extra. A $25 million advertising campaign will herald the name change. Another $100 million will be spent to switch signs at the company's more than 25,000 stations and impart Exxon to its letterheads, gas pumps and trucks.

The name is the product of more than five years of linguistic analysis, psychological testing of consumers, and test marketing (TIME, Oct. 25). Humble researchers examined thousands of computer-chosen alphabetic combinations and words in 55 languages until they found one that seemed to stick in consumers' minds and had no obscene or embarrassing meanings in any foreign tongue. A major breakthrough was the finding that there is no word with a double X in any language except Maltese. Since the new trademark might eventually be used by Jersey Standard overseas, one of its present labels, Enco, was an early reject. It means "stalled car" in Japanese.

Übersetzung auf Seite 118

Vocabulary

bar v.	prevent, stop
brandish v.	flourish, display
entail v.	involve, be accompanied by
grapple v.	struggle
herald v.	announce, publish, make known
impart to v.	put on, adorn, deck out, bring to
label n.	name, trademark
operating arm	branch office
researcher n.	investigator
"stall a car"	„Motor abwürgen"
switch v.	exchange

Questions on the text

1. Do you know any brand names given at the beginning of the article and if so, can you say which products they represent?
2. What were the consequences of the 1911 breakup of the old Standard Oil trust as far as the trademark Esso is concerned?
3. What are the costs involved in the change of Humble's brand name?
4. What research was carried out by Humble to find the new name?
5. Why did the company finally agree on the name Exxon?

Points for discussion

1. Suggest reasons why companies sometimes find it necessary to change their trademarks.
2. Discuss how a product's image influences its sales.
3. Advertising is an item of expenditure. Why do companies advertise at all?
4. State your personal opinion on Humble's choice of the name Exxon.

Facing the economic facts of life

The annual currency crisis is subsiding amid the usual recriminations, the usual calls for new rules to prevent speculation, and the usual arguments about gold and paper assets and the relative wickedness of countries which export too many goods or too much money. Because these arguments are so usual, there is a temptation to commit them to some limbo of unutterable boredom, and assume that everything will stagger on much as before. After so many incomprehensible alarms, even those closely concerned find it hard to realise that this time it is different; this time the situation really is dangerous.

The most pressing and apparent danger is the protectionist mood of the US Congress, and its hostility to President Nixon. President Nixon can only negotiate on trade matters when he is armed with authority from Congress; Congress appears willing only to issue a two-edged weapon, which can be used to cut trade as well as to cut barriers—and the President himself is perfectly willing to use threats as well as peace offers in order to get his trading partners into serious negotiations. There is a danger that trade issues are about to be Vietnamised.

It is easy to react to this threat with outraged anti-Americanism, and that reaction was already apparent in Brussels last week. But American impatience is not altogether unreasonable. It is on this side of the Atlantic that it does not seem to be realised that we face problems which are not likely to yield to a few technical monetary devices and some haggling over the trade rules. New rules will not abolish the logic which dictates that money is going to remain mobile simply because trade and business organisations have become international; that as long as inflation remains an unsolved problem, there will be uncertainty over money values; and that large and persistent imbalances in trade reflect structural faults which evidently do not disappear at the stroke of a money-changer's pen.

We really face two choices: to learn to live with these problems for the years which it will take to find radical solutions, or to abolish them by retreating, along one route or another, into increasing trade and monetary isolation. Each country seems able to see the problem in its own terms: Britain rightly argues that the pound cannot be repegged until we have stabilised costs at home; Japan, with equal justice, points out that her unbalanced trade reflects an unbalanced economy, which must be redirected from industrial to welfare expansion. But we are impatient with the problems of others—the French with the British float, the whole world with the "threat" of Japan's excellent consumer goods.

If these problems are to be solved, they must be recognised. We need a monetary system which will not be overturned by unavoidable uncertainties; agreement on how persistent imbalances are to be financed and in the longer run, corrected; agreement, as the Americans have argued, on what kind of temporary protection for infant and declining industries is legitimate; and agreement on the disciplines under which multi-national companies should operate. What we seem to be getting is old remedies for money problems, hostile manoeuvres over trade, and a refusal to face at all the long-term problems of structure, energy supplies, and defence burdens which lie behind the crises. Britain, with the most open of economies, should be the first to take the strategic view and tell its partners that economic maladjustment cannot be tackled by people who behave like maladjusted children.

Übersetzung auf Seite 120

Vocabulary

amid	in the middle of
assets (pl.) n.	Vermögenswerte, Aktiva (opposite: liabilities)
devices (pl.) n.	Instrumentarium
float, British float	here: the fact that the pound sterling is floating at the moment
haggle v.	argue, dispute
hostility n.	Feindseligkeit, Unfreundlichkeit

incomprehensible	not to be understood
issue n.	problem
limbo n. ('lɪmbɔu)	place for forgotten and unwanted things
maladjusted ('mælə'dʒʌstid)	unable to adapt oneself properly to one's environment
maladjustment n.	hier etwa: Fehlverhalten
outraged ('autreidʒd)	angry, extreme
overturn v.	turn upside down
peg v.	keep steady (e.g. pegged exchange rates = feste Wechselkurse)
persistent	recurring, permanent
prevent v.	hinder, stop
protectionist mood	willingness to protect (guard) home industry against foreign competition by levying taxes on imports
recrimination n.	accusation on a mutual basis
stagger v.	stumble
stroke n.	here: single movement
subside v.	here: to become quiet(er)
temptation n.	Versuchung
two-edged	with two edges, with two sharp cutting parts
unavoidable	inevitable
wickedness n. (from: wicked)	immoral, bad, wrong attitude or action
yield to v.	here: be solved by

Questions on the text

1. Why does the writer of the article think that this annual currency crisis is different from others?
2. What does President Nixon need for trade negotiations?
3. What is meant by the word "Vietnamised"?
4. According to the author, what are the two possible ways the countries mentioned could take?

5. Why is Britain not willing to fix the exchange rate of the pound sterling?
6. Are there any suggestions in the text on how to solve the problems mentioned?
7. What role is Britain expected to play?

Points for discussion

1. Discuss how, in your opinion, the currency crisis could be solved.
2. What consequences would American protectionism have
    a) for the United States itself?
    b) for other countries?
3. Trade and business organisations have become more international. What does this mean for
    a) the organisations themselves?
    b) trade and marketing?
    c) the economy as a whole?
4. Describe a monetary system you think most suited to solve the present day problems.

How to Fight Inflation

The problem of inflation, from which no industrial country is at present free, is a political problem. The reason that there is worldwide inflation is not that economic theory can offer no way of maintaining the value of a currency, but that the policies required to maintain the value of currencies are not acceptable to democratic electorates and create intolerable political pressures even for authoritarian regimes....

The great effect of inflation is that it produces a transfer of purchasing power. People talk very freely about the cost of inflation, about the way in which they have to pay more for their meat or bread or houses. People do not talk so freely about the way in which they personally benefit from inflation, though inflation would not continue if very powerful groups in our society did not benefit from it. If everyone were genuinely against inflation, as almost everyone professes to be, then the political pressures which operate against stable currencies would not exist and it would be a relatively simple matter to ensure price stability in the western world....

As inflation is a political problem it can only be resolved by political means. It creates the greatest possible difficulties for any government. The electorate greatly resent rising prices, but they also resent the measures, whether of deflation or of incomes policy, which are designed to stop prices rising. If a country has experienced a run-away inflation, as Germany did in the 1920s, then the public feeling against inflation may be strong enough to allow a government to act consistently in the interests of price stability. That could happen here, but it has not happened yet.

Normally, however, once inflation has reached the present level, a government is faced with an extremely unpleasant choice. If it allows prices to continue to rise then it can expect to lose the next election on the prices issue. If it pursues sufficiently severe policies to reduce the rate at which prices rise, let alone create monetary stability, then it can expect to lose the next election on the issue of unemployment. The Labour Government failed to solve this problem, and indeed ended up firmly impaled on both horns of its dilemma. The present government is in a position of even greater difficulty with a more pressing inflation and a higher existing level of unemployment.

The Prime Minister is no doubt quite right to say that there is no miracle ingredient called an incomes policy which will solve this dilemma for him. In any case, the ability to have an incomes policy depends on the political situation of the Government and on its political relations with the trade unions and with the mass of trade unionists. That does not however mean that statutory regulation of wages and prices has nothing to offer as part of a general policy for containing inflation.

What is strange is that the Government has neither had an incomes nor a monetary policy, although these are the two classic alternatives for combating inflation. It is essential that a government should have a general strategy towards inflation; in our view that strategy should include the use of different weapons precisely because no individual policy can be decisive by itself.

The run-away monetary policy of the past twelve months has gone beyond what was valuable in expanding demand and reducing unemployment, and has indeed so far been unsuccessful in restoring industrial confidence. Between 1969 and early 1970 monetary policy was almost certainly too severe. In the past year it has even more certainly been too relaxed. ...

The Government should have tried to have as much influence in the area of incomes policy as it could obtain.

... A statutory incomes policy with powers to delay unreasonable settlement, and powers to impose temporary freezes or cooling off periods when inflation becomes particularly severe, ought to be a normal part of national economic policy. Cooperation between a reasonably restrained monetary policy, voluntary cooperation with industry such as the Government has achieved with the CBI, and an incomes policy which has limited but definite statutory powers offers the best prospect of mitigating the inflationary evil. Such policies must be supported by other policies of social justice, and if possible economic growth, which restores the feeling of national equity which inflation destroys.

The basic political difficulty would nevertheless remain. The forces in society which tend to promote inflation are very strong. In most countries they appear at present to be stronger than a democratic government facing a vigorous opposition and needing to win elections. In some countries they are stronger than authoritarian regimes which have to cope with the strains and pressures of politics just as much as does a democratic government. The best we can hope for in these circumstances is a prudent, supple and wily fighting retreat designed to reduce the damage and the rate of inflation and not conducted with any illusions about the possibility of great victories. ...

Übersetzung auf Seite 122

Vocabulary

allow v.	permit
benefit n.	profit
confidence n.	Vertrauen
contain v.	keep under control or within limits
cope with v.	manage successfully
create v.	cause
currency n.	the official medium of exchange or money of a country, money that is actually in use in a country
delay v.	postpone, put off until later
deflation n.	a situation in which the value of the monetary unit is rising as a result of falling prices
elector n.	person having the right to vote
electorate n.	all those who can vote
equity n. ('ekwɪtɪ)	fairness
face v.	confront
genuine ('dʒenjuɪn)	true
impale v.	pin down, pierce with a sharp-pointed stake or spear
issue n.	question for discussion, problem
let alone v.	not to mention

43

miracle ingredient	Wundermittel, Allheilmittel
mitigate v.	make less severe or painful
monetary policy	Währungspolitik
pressure n.	force exerted continuously on or against sth.
profess v. (prɔ'fes)	claim
purchase v. ('pə:tʃəs)	buy
purchasing power	Kaufkraft
pursue v. (pə:sju:)	go on with
resent v. (rɪ'zent)	show or feel indignation at
retreat v./n.	go back
rising prices	increasing prices
run-away inflation (also: galloping inflation)	galoppierende Inflation
statute n.	law passed by Parliament or other law-making body
statutory	law-making, given by law
supple	quick to respond, adaptable
trade union	Gewerkschaft
trade unionist	Gewerkschaftler
unemployment n.	Arbeitslosigkeit
value n.	Wert
vigorous	strong
wile n.	trick, cunning procedure
wily (waɪlɪ)	full of wishes

Questions on the text

1. What causes the author to consider the problem of inflation a political problem?
2. Has inflation any effect on the purchasing power?
3. If everyone were against inflation, would that help to ensure price stability?
4. Which measures are designed to stop prices rising?
5. How do you explain the term "run-away inflation"?
6. Why is there a strong public feeling against inflation in West Germany?

7. In what respect are inflation and unemployment linked with each other?
8. What role do the trade unions play?
9. What, in the author's view, should be a normal part of national economic policy?
10. What do you think is meant when the article speaks of "forces in society which tend to promote inflation"?

Points for discussion

1. Compare the rate of inflation in Great Britain with other European countries. Try to find reasons for the differences.
2. Discuss some of the numerous economic consequences if prices rise and/or fall.
3. Analyse how far the system of fixed exchange rates influences the national money value.
4. Which rate of wage increase, in your opinion, does not affect the value of money? Why?
5. Point out the influence of government expenditure on the rate of inflation.

Bonn hopes to deflate the boom

The West German Government this week announced a series of tax increases as part of a programme which is designed to reduce purchasing power by some £840 millions.

From July petrol tax will be increased by five pfennigs a litre (about 3p per gallon). This will put West Germany second in the European table of petrol prices. A litre of normal grade petrol will cost 72 pfennigs here compared with the Italian equivalent of 85 pfennigs, and slightly higher than the cost in France.

Income tax paid by the well-off is also to be raised. For a year from July 1 unmarried people with a taxable income of more than DM100,000 (about £14,000), and married couples whose taxable income is at least twice that amount will have to pay an extra 10 per cent tax. This revenue will be "frozen" for the time being and later used for a new type of scheme to help people acquire assets.

The Government is also to float a loan with a total value of about £560 millions which will be deposited with the Federal Reserve Bank. The idea is to reduce the amount of money in circulation and so to curb inflation.

At a meeting on Saturday the Cabinet approved a Budget for 1973 of DM120,000 millions (about £16,800 millions). This is an increase of 9.7 per cent on this year's inflation.

Übersetzung auf Seite 125

Vocabulary

acquire v.	gain, get
approve v. (ə'pru:v)	agree to, accept
assets (pl.) n.	Vermögenswerte, Aktiva (opposite: liabilities)
curb inflation	die Inflation eindämmen

designed	planned, intended
Federal Reserve Bank	Deutsche Bundesbank
float a loan	hier: Stabilitätsanleihe auflegen
"frozen"	eingefroren; hier: stillgelegt
money in circulation	Geldumlauf, Bargeldumlauf
purchasing power	Kaufkraft
revenue n.	income; Ertrag
tax n.	amount of money levied by the government or state
well-off	rich

Questions on the text

1. What is the aim of the West German Government's new programme?
2. What kinds of taxes will be increased?
3. Is the tax on petrol high and what can you say about the petrol prices in Germany if you compare them with those in other European countries?
4. Will income tax be increased generally?
5. What will the German Government use the revenue they will gain from tax increases for?
6. What is the idea behind the Government's plan to float a loan?
7. Why is the Federal Reserve Bank mentioned in this article?

Points for discussion

1. Describe the role of the Federal Reserve Bank in the attempt to curb inflation.
2. Try to outline the relationship between Central Bank and Government.
3. Will the steps taken by the German Government as described in the article be sufficient to curb inflation? Give reasons for your opinion.

A Secret IMF Proposal for Monetary Reform Urges Radical Changes

Washington—There's no mystery about what's holding up earnest talks on international monetary reform, Treasury Secretary John B. Connally contends. It is the lack of a "clue" to what other nations want.

But now more than a clue has appeared—it's a fairly detailed proposal, in the form of a closely guarded internal memorandum of the 120-country International Monetary Fund.

The proposal, drafted by the IMF staff, is getting generally favorable attention as it circulates confidentially among embassies here and key finance ministries around the world. But by the authors' own admission, it will strike some countries as "both radical and inconvenient."

The country most likely to take that view is the U.S. because the IMF document includes the stern messages that the U.S.:

—Can no longer let dollars pile up abroad and must buy back dollars that flow out in the future with gold or other assets by definite deadlines.

—Should be as prepared as any other nation promptly to devalue the dollar again (or revalue upward) as conditions change.

—Should expect to see tens of billions of dollars now held by other governments turned in to the IMF—and gradually to buy them back.

—Must get over the ideas that other nations will be made to give up their balance-of-payments surpluses and that gold will soon fade from its place as an international reserve asset.

What the IMF proposal omits may well be what makes it most objectionable to the Nixon administration. It leaves out any "sanctions" to pressure other nations into ridding themselves swiftly of payments surpluses so that the U.S. needn't try too hard to wipe out its deficits.

Even in the U.S., however, various elements of the IMF proposal are welcome in various quarters. Administration officials, though keeping quiet about it for fear of stirring currency-market speculation, generally concur that further dollar devaluations should be a relatively routine tool for improving trade balances in the future. Although the U.S. need not "agree with its every point," the IMF document "is a good place to start" reform negotiations, says Democratic Rep. Henry Reuss, ... head of the international unit of the Joint Economic Committee. Some strategists add that the mechanics of this or almost any other known approach probably could work if other countries would take the trade, tax and other steps necessary to help the U.S. pull out of its perennial payments deficits.

The broad purpose of the IMF plan isn't controversial. It seeks to replace the currency exchange system hastily worked out at the Smithsonian Institution in Dec., 1971 with one designed to last "for the next 15 to 20 years."...

But the sense of urgency invoked by the IMF report is controversial, at least to the Nixon administration. The Smithsonian rules —under which other countries go on accumulating dollars without any promise of convertibility into gold or other assets—"do not reflect economic and political realities," the report says. It warns that continuation of the present rules risks an unplanned "separation of the world into a number of currency blocs with ... attendant economic and political hazards."...

The IMF ideas are "not dissimilar" to the British government's views, a diplomat says; both emphasize a sharply declining role for the dollar in official international dealings. Instead of the U.S.'s or any other nation's money, governments would use a souped-up model of the "special drawing rights" created by the IMF as the main form of international financial reserve.

The IMF proposal would go further than the British have gone in public statements, however. In something of a final stripping of privileged status from the dollar, the report suggests that even the dollar's role as the main "intervention currency," be ended ...

Instead, the IMF tentatively proposes "symmetrical multicurrency intervention."...

The document declares, the change "would completely eliminate the special position of the dollar" for other participants. But because it would be "a very sharp break from past practices," the report adds that other reforms might have to be pushed through first.

Such a blow at the dollar's stature might get ample support in international monetary circles. Many foreigners resent the way the U.S. has let dollars build up abroad, worsening their inflation problems...

But the purpose of a new "intervention" scheme would be more than just revenge. Rather, the IMF reasoning goes, such a scheme would be the final step into an era in which other nations would no longer depend on chancy U.S. payments deficits for growth in their monetary reserves. Strategists say the proposed plan would be more orderly and would enhance the IMF's role as a sort of world central bank rationally creating extra SDRs for reserve growth.

Thus, the IMF planners wouldn't want to see any upstart currency, such as one of the European Common Market countries might ultimately create, usurping the reserve role. "A potentially dangerous expansion" of some "emerging" reserve currencies is already a threat, the report cautions. Many analysts agree that whenever a nation acts as banker for other governments there's the risk of a panicky breakdown if too many want to remove their deposits at the same time.

Ironically, the report finds, what has passed for a monetary system since August 15 is "more dollar-centered than ever before". Other governments still absorb dollars in order to hold currency values relatively steady, but now they do it without any U.S. pledge to redeem the dollars in gold. The dollar holdings of foreign governments were $47.9 billion at the end of January 1972, up from $33 billion last July and $20 billion at the close of January 1971.

To remove that existing "overhang" of foreign-held dollars, the report proposes giving other nations "the option (and perhaps up to a point the obligation) to turn these balances into SDRs" through what it calls "consolidation arrangements." Basically, these would have the IMF absorb the dollars in return for a big new issue of SDRs.

To keep these foreigners' dollar holdings from swelling indefinitely, the IMF report proposes annual or even quarterly compulsory conversion." That means that if Germany were to accumulate $500 million in U.S. dollars in three months' time, for instance, the U.S. Treasury would face a firm deadline for coughing up a like amount of gold, SDRs or other currencies to buy them back. To meet its obligation, the U.S. might have to borrow from other nations or from the IMF.

The report concedes that the U.S. can't be expected to agree to such "asset financing" of its payments deficits "unless it could count on exchange-rate policy as one means of curing deficits." Now that Congress has enacted President Nixon's request for devaluation of the dollar—raising the price of gold to $38 an ounce from $35—"parity changes of the U.S. dollar have become an acknowledged part of the exchange-rate mechanism," the report says. All that remains to be done on this score is for the IMF to formalize future flexibility for the value of the dollar and all other currencies.

Übersetzung auf Seite 126

Vocabulary

adopt v.	vote to accept, take and use
asset n. (usually pl. = assets)	anything owned by a person, company, etc. that has money value and that may be sold to pay debts
caution v.	warn
clue n. (kluː)	fact, idea, that suggests a possible answer to a problem
cough up v.	get sth. out of the throat; ausspucken
deadline n.	fixed limit of time
devalue v.	reduce the value of the home currency in terms of foreign currency
enhance v. (ınˈhaːns)	add to; vergrößern, erhöhen
exchange rate	Wechselkurs

hazard n. ('hæzəd)	risk, danger
IMF	International Monetary Fund; Internationaler Währungsfond; a Special Agency of the UNO with headquarters in Washington
margin n.	Bandbreite
object v.	be opposed to, make a protest against
objectionable	likely to be objected to
option n.	right or power of choosing
perennial	lasting for a very long time, permanent
pile up v.	form into a heap, accumulate
pledge n.	promise
reedem v.	get back by payment
revenge n. (rɪ'vendʒ)	deliberate infliction of injury upon the person from whom injury has been received
rid v.	make free (of)
SDR	Special Drawing Rights; Sondererziehungsrechte
souped-up	"wieder aufpoliert"
stern	demanding and enforcing obedience, severe, strict
stir v.	cause to move
surplus n.	amount of money that remains after needs have been supplied, excess of receipts over expenditure; Überschuß
trade balance or balance of trade	the current account section of the balance of payments; Handelsbilanz

Questions on the text

1. Which are the most important points of the IMF memorandum?
2. Why is the U.S. administration likely to be opposed to the IMF proposal?

3. What are the British government's views on the role of the dollar?
4. Which are the main consequences resulting from a continuation of the Smithsonian rules?
5. In what does the author of the article see the attack on the dollar's stature?
6. What is meant by "consolidation arrangements"?
7. What does the IMF report propose to keep the foreign countries' dollar holdings from swelling indefinitely?

Points for discussion
1. Discuss the problem of devaluing a currency.
2. State your opinion about the role of the IMF as a sort of world central bank.
3. Point out the advantages and disadvantages of the dollar
   a) as a reserve currency,
   b) as an intervention currency.
4. Explain the difference between fixed exchange rates and floating exchange rates.

What Marshall Aid did for Europe

It has been a bad year for Marshall Aid. The 25 years that separate us from United States Secretary of State George Marshall's Harvard speech have witnessed a process of steady expansion of American economic and military power, followed by a seemingly inevitable process of declining economic leverage and moral humiliation.

In South-east Asia the Marshall Aid syndrome, as Professor Galbraith calls it—messianic intervention backed by limitless funds—nears a dramatic climax. In Western Europe the reversal in trading patterns away from dollar supremacy has now reached a critical point, a watershed in international trade that questions on simple tactical grounds the soundness for the United States of Washington's cold war strategies after 1945.

Survivors of the Marshal Aid years in Washington must look back with conflicting sentiments over the developments of the past 25 years. The aim of Marshall and many of his senior advisers, to isolate the "communist" states of Europe through destroying the traditional pattern of European trade, nevertheless promoted in Western Europe both a growing revulsion against dollar power and a surge towards economic integration as a means of eliminating that power.

Marshall Aid helped emasculate the economies of Eastern Europe; it also launched Western Europe on an expansionary course that now threatens the United States commercial position at its roots. There must be analysts in Washington who now question both the magnitude of aid under the Marshall Plan and the divisive doctrine that accompanied it, for its funds have produced a serious economic rival and its uncompromising anticommunist bias generated an eventual union of 10 of the Continent's most dynamic states.

In 1947, Western Europe faced a massive trade deficit on current account, and a $1,500 m deficiency on capital account. Despite

$6,000 m in United States funds West European currency reserves fell $2,500 m over the year. At the Paris conference a four-year payments deficit of $22,000 m was projected for up to 1952. The European Recovery Programme was designed to fill this payments gap; Congress earmarked over $5,000 m for the first year of its operation.

Following the launching of ERP dollar trade steadily replaced pan-European trade and the European economy was split into two, a division made permanent with the emergence of the European Community. The basic criterion for allocating funds under ERP was, for each country, "the prospective size of its deficit with the dollar area."

Inherent in this formula, therefore, was encouragement of trade with the dollar block, since the bigger the deficit on dollar account the larger could be the national claim for ERP allocation. Between 1947 and 1950 United States aid paid for 25 per cent of Western Europe's total imports and nearly 70 per cent of these imports came from the dollar area.

Of the 1947 current account deficit of $7,000 m more than $5,000 m sprang from imports from the United States. Under ERP this dollar deficit was to be reduced by dollar aid, but since currency shortage was the critical problem Western European exports needed to go to areas where currency for payment was plentiful, that is to the United States. Consequently, between 1947 and 1957 Western European exports to the dollar area leapt by 400 per cent.

More seriously, the political rationale of American aid policy—supported by congressional requirements banning trade with communist regimes—stifled any prospect of improved trade with Eastern Europe and laid the ground work for commercial division of the Continent.

BY 1955, the cold war in economics seemed won. Eastern Europe had been isolated. Western Europe had come close to being a commercial extension of the United States. British trade was centred firmly on dollar exports, Western Europe had become Atlantic-minded.

As a corollary to this process, dollar investment in Western Europe exploded: in 1950 it was $118,000 m, by 1963 had reached $406,000 m, an expansion of 244 per cent in 13 years. America's challenge to communism had become a challenge to Western Europe.

From 1958, the founding year of EEC, this movement has been startling. In 1958 only 30 per cent of EEC trade was among member states; in 1971 for the first time over half its trade was entirely internal. British entry will add crucially to this trend: since 1958 British trade with Western Europe has soared by 300 per cent, a momentum that will further accelerate with the gradual elimination of barriers.

United States sales to EEC actually fell in 1971, despite an 11 per cent expansion in EEC imports as a whole. As the enlarged EEC becomes more self-sufficient in foodstuffs and technology the volume of United States imports will diminish, all adding truth to the remark offered to assembled Congress recently by Professor Richard Cooper of Yale: "The European Community has by far the largest trade with the rest of the world, and by historical precedent the mantle of leadership should pass to it."

Übersetzung auf Seite 130

Vocabulary

allocate v.	give, distribute
Atlantic-minded	here: orientated towards the United States
bias ('baɪəs) n.	leaning towards or away from sth., here: prejudice
challenge (to) n.	Herausforderung, Kampfansage
climax n.	highest point
corollary n.	natural result, natural consequence
Cooper, Richard N.	am. Wirtschaftswissenschaftler
crucially	here: enormously and seriously
deficiency n.	shortage, lack
divisive	from: divide

earmark v.	bereitstellen, bewilligen (für einen bestimmten Zweck)
emasculate v.	weaken
humiliation n.	Demütigung, Erniedrigung
inevitable	unavoidable
inherent	existing in sth. as a natural part or element of it
Galbreith, John Kenneth	am. Nationalökonom und Politiker, geb. 1908
launch on a course	set in the direction
leap (leapt) v.	increase, jump rapidly upward
leverage n.	here: power, manoeuverability
magnitude n.	enormous size, amount
mantle n.	here: symbol
Marshall Aid	Marshallplanhilfe — auf Anregung von George C. Marshall, 1880—1959. am. General und Politiker, 1947—49 Außenminister der USA —; auch: Europ. Wiederaufbauprogramm, Hilfswerk der USA zur wirtschaftlichen Unterstützung der westeuropäischen Länder nach dem 2. Weltkrieg
messianic	from Messiah — Jesus Christ, the Saviour
momentum n.	impulse, impetus
promote v.	here: evoke
rationale n.	logical basis
reversal n. (from: reverse v.)	turning the other way round
revulsion n.	Abneigung
startling	amazing
stifle v.	suppress
soar v.	go up high, increase
seemingly inevitable	apparently unavoidable
surge n.	rapid movement
trading pattern	Handelsstruktur
witness v.	see

Questions on the text
1. What does the expression "Marshall Aid" mean?
2. Is there any connection between "Marshall Aid" and ERP?
3. What was Marshall aiming at when he proposed his plan in 1947?
4. Has this goal been achieved?
5. Did US Congress have a decisive influence on ERP?
6. How were the funds under ERP allocated?
7. Was the trade between the European countries and the dollar block affected by the allocation of ERP-funds?
8. Marshall aid was not given to the countries of Eastern Europe. Why?
9. What is the reason for the decline in US sales to EEC in 1971?

Points for discussion
1. Analyse why especially in Western Europe the dollar supremacy has now reached such a critical point.
2. Do you think that the aid given under the Marshall Plan and the inherent anticommunist tendency of the latter has had any effect on the founding of the Common Market?
3. Discuss Mr. Cooper's statement that the mantle of leadership should pass to the EEC because it has the largest trade with the rest of the world.
4. Compare the trading pattern in Western and Eastern Europe after World War II.

The Year of the Grand Disillusion

By the time Henry Kissinger takes the oath as Secretary of State, only a few months will remain in what he once optimistically proclaimed as "the Year of Europe." So far there has been almost no progress toward the goal he set for this year—a redefinition and reaffirmation of the principles binding together the Atlantic community. Part of this delay has been caused by Western Europe's own increasing disunity. Despite the unprecedented ease with which Western European nations send goods across each other's borders, the European Economic Community seethes with some of the deepest discontent in its 15-year history.

Most alarming is the steady deterioration of relations between Paris and Bonn. It flared into the open this month when Jacques Chirac, France's Minister of Agriculture and a close confidant of President Georges Pompidou, complained that "I am concerned by the way that Germany is turning away from Europe." West German Chancellor Willy Brandt attempted to cool the exchange, dismissing Chirac's remarks as the mutterings of a low-level official. But some of the Chancellor's colleagues have privately retaliated, charging that "the French are suffering from gaps of logic. They cry and protest like small children."

Such bickering has exacerbated the strained relations between Pompidou and Brandt. It is an open secret in Paris that Pompidou distrusts Brandt's government. The French leader worries that the increased influence wielded by the extreme left within Brandt's Social Democratic Party may make the Chancellor a less reliable partner in keeping Western Europe militarily secure. He also believes that the German government is more concerned with its Ostpolitik policy of normalizing relations with the Communist regimes of Eastern Europe than with solving the problems of Western Europe. A Pompidou aide muses: "The EEC is confining for Germany. What would be the German reaction in five years if the Soviets offered them reunification?" The French answer their own question. The Germans "would pack up their dossier and return to Bonn," drop out of the Common Market and become a "neutral" as the price for getting back East Germany.

Ridiculous Fears. Brandt's aides call the French fears "ridiculous." They declare that the West German government has no intention of turning neutral. They also point out that West Germany could not economically afford to leave the EEC. The real culprit, they say, is Paris, whose obfuscations and petty legalisms have stalled progress in the EEC for so long. Furthermore, if the French distrust Bonn's motives, the West Germans are equally convinced that France once more is developing serious domestic weaknesses. "The problems of French policy," says a senior Brandt adviser, "stem from an internal situation in which there is no majority for anything—European or national. Nothing is stable in that country since De Gaulle left. French politicians are in a political and economic state where nobody knows where they are going."

Especially galling to the West Germans is French opposition to a reform of the EEC's Common Agricultural Policy, or CAP, as it is called, which gives heavy subsidies to France's farmers. Already Bonn's payments to the agricultural fund exceed $1 billion annually. "The goal was to have achieved monetary and economic union by 1980," says a West German official. "Now, seven years from that goal, where are we? The British and the Germans are paying for French agriculture. That is all, and that is not enough." Remarked German Foreign Minister Walter Scheel last week: "This objective (of union by 1980) will never be achieved if each of the interested parties says: 'L'Europe, c'est moi.'"

It was hoped that the British entry this year into the Common Market—blocked for twelve years by the French—would inject a renewed sense of purpose that would encourage a compromise between France and Germany. But now, according to The Netherlands' Prime Minister Joop den Uyl, "there is a feeling of disappointment. All the problems have come back within the enlarged Community." For this reason, many Britons are already voicing second thoughts about their long-debated decision to "join Europe."

The introduction of the Market's 10% value-added tax on all goods and services has irritated the British consumer, who is attempting to cope with an 8.4% inflation rate. Imports from the

Continent, such as Italian refrigerators, French cars and German leather goods, have flowed into England faster than British exports have gone to other EEC members. In the meantime, the Market has not yet acted on programs that would directly benefit Britain, such as investing in its industrially underdeveloped regions. It is no wonder that a recent Gallup poll in Britain revealed that 52 % of those queried now feel that their nation erred in joining the Market. The widespread British popular dissatifsaction with the EEC will almost certainly pressure London into assuming a tougher posture toward its Common Market partners. None of this bodes well for Kissinger's Europe policy. He had hoped that the Sept. 10—11 meeting of the EEC's foreign ministers in Copenhagen would result in a joint platform representing a unified European viewpoint on the future political and military functions of the Atlantic Alliance. The changes of that now seem slim. At best, the foreign ministers may only be able to agree on how and in what forum the members of the EEC will receive President Richard Nixon if he visits Europe this autumn as expected. If the bickering continues, some Germans gloomily predict, by 1980 Europe will be little more than a glorified supermarket filled with Common Market goods.

Übersetzung auf Seite 133

Vocabulary

bicker v.	quarrel
bode (well) v.	foresee, forecast; von (guter) Vorbedeutung sein
confining	restricting
cope with v.	accept
culprit n.	troublemaker
delay n.	postponement
deterioration n. (from: deteriorate)	worsening
dossier n. ('dɔsɪeɪ)	Akten, Unterlagen
encourage v. (ɪn'kʌrɪdʒ)	support
exacerbate v. (eks'æsəbeɪt)	make worse
exceed v.	go beyond, surpass
flare v.	here: burst

61

galling	disturbing, aggravating
gloomy	dismal, sullen
goal n.	aim, objective
muse v.	comment
obfuscation n.	obscuration, obscurities,
(from: obfuscate)	camouflage
posture n.	position
predict v.	forecast, say in advance
query v. ('kwıərı)	ask, question
reliable	dependable
retaliate v.	take revenge
second thought	opinion reached after reconsideration
seethe v.	be agitated, boil
slim	small
stem from v.	arise from
subsidy n.	money granted; Subventionen
take the oath	den Eid ablegen
unprecedented	never done or known before
value-added tax (abbr. VAT)	Mehrwertsteuer
wield v.	exert, hold

Questions on the text

1. Why has there been no progress achieved in what Henry Kissinger proclaimed as "the Year of Europe"?
2. What is said about German-French relations?
3. What does France blame Germany for?
4. Why does Pompidou distrust Brandt's government?
5. How do the French believe the Germans would act if they were offered reunification by the Soviets?
6. How have the French prevented progress according to German opinion?
7. What, in the German point of view, is the main problem of French policy?
8. Why do the French oppose a reform of the EEC's CAP?
9. What is in Walter Scheel's opinion the main obstacle to monetary and economic union?
10. Why are many Britons dissatisfied with the EEC?

Points for discussion
1. Do you think that there is a real danger of German neutrality? Support your answer.
2. Is in your opinion Britain's entry into the EEC advantageous for
   a) Britain herself,
   b) the Community?
3. Discuss the chances of the EEC to achieve the goal of a monetary and economic union by 1980.
4. What role do you see for the United States of America in Europe?

More cultural contacts in Europe

Britain is planning to spend an additional £6 million over the next four years on a programme to increase her cultural contacts with other European countries. The programme will not be confined to the traditional areas of education and the arts. It also encompasses youth exchanges, exchanges of young workers, exchange between women's organisations and an increase in town-twinning. There are plans to set up a European Discussion Centre in the United Kingdom alongside the existing Wilton Park Conference Centre, and it is hoped that a British Cultural Centre will be established in Paris. Increased attention will be given to language teaching.

The programme was announced on March 6 by the Chancellor of the Duchy of Lancaster, Mr Geoffrey Rippon, in a written parliamentary reply. The initiative comes at a moment when Britain is in the final stages of her preparations for membership of the enlarged European Community and can be seen as evidence of the new "European" thinking that now prevails. Although most of the money will be spent on increasing contacts with countries in the Community, some of the items in the programme will involve the Council of Europe, which embraces other countries of Western Europe.

Possibly the most interesting item in the programme is the Government's offer of fifty fellowships a year to post-graduates from Western Europe for study at British universities. It is the Government's hope that other European countries will follow up this initiative by offering reciprocal scholarships at their universities for British post-graduates.

Of the £6 million to be spent, £3½ million will be used to expand the activities of the British Council. In addition, to the fellowship scheme, the Council will play a major role in the promotion of British books, in increased cooperation between European libraries, in the creation of science and technology information units in certain countries, in improving links between universities, and in the promotion of exchanges and meetings between members of the professions and specialists.

Some of the money for the new programme will be provided by the Department of Education and Science for such projects as: assisting teachers from other countries to attend the Department's short courses for teachers; developing in the United Kingdom a European Centre for Information on current research in modern language teaching; helping the Royal Society to double the number of fellowships made under the Western European Scientific Interchange Programme; and the promotion of exchanges between young workers.

Übersetzung auf Seite 135

Vocabulary

Chancellor of the Duchy of Lancaster	hier: Europaminister
confined to	restricted to, limited to
current	here: present
embrace v.	include
encompass v. (ınˈkʌmpəs)	encircle, include
evidence n.	proof
fellowship n.	Stipendium (zur Erlangung eines höheren akademischen Grades)
involve v.	here: concern, touch
prevail v.	reign
provide v.	give, supply
scholarship n.	Forschungsstipendium
set up v.	found, establish
town-twinning	Gründung von Partnerschaften zwischen Städten

Questions on the text

1. What does the new British programme for increasing cultural contacts with Europe include?
2. Where and by whom was this programme announced?
3. Is the programme intended for members of the EC only?

4. What does the author consider to be the most interesting item of the programme?
5. Which are the main fields of the British Council's activities?
6. What does the Department of Education finance?

Points for discussion

1. Increased attention will be given to language teaching. Can you see special reasons for this?
2. Do you think more intense cultural contacts contribute essentially to a unified Europe?
3. What functions, in your opinion, do the representatives of a country in other countries, such as embassies or the British Council, fulfil?
4. The exchange of people under a cultural programme is nothing but concealed tourism. Discuss.
5. Given the restricted number of university places, would you be in favour of accepting foreign students at the universities in this country? Give reasons for your answer.

European Road Construction

Increase in Length of Roads

This report deals with the growth in construction of motorways and major national trunk roads in Western Europe, primarily in the European Economic Community and the European Free Trade Association.

At the end of World War II, only Germany, with over 2000 km (1250 miles) of motorways constructed between 1933 and 1942, had any recognizable motorway network. By 1953 both Italy and Holland had begun building motorways and this type of road reached 2700 km in Europe in that year. Between 1953 and 1963 the length of motorways increased by over 9 % a year, reaching about 6600 km. By 1967 the length was extended to over 10,000 km, an annnual growth rate of 12 %. In that year West Germany had the most developed motorway network, followed by Italy, France, and the U.K. The country with the fastest growing network was France; the U.K. came next.

Throughout Europe the construction of completely new major national roads other than motorways is on a much restricted scale. The major efforts are concentrated on motorway construction and on providing by-passes to badly congested areas.

Passenger Traffic

Even though the length of motorways is expected almost to treble between 1967 and 1980, the addition will not be adequate to meet the need of the greater number of vehicles on the road. In large measure, new construction and improvement of old roads will stimulate even greater automobile usage. It is estimated that a new motorway adds an extra 20 % in mileage driven to the normal traffic flow, and 50 % to tourist traffic. However, a large increase in annual average mileage traveled by private cars is not expected. Because of the greater congestion on the roads and sharper competition from low-cost package tour operators, tourists will tend to use air transport rather than the road network for destinations farther from the main tourist generating countries. Businessmen will rely more heavily on air transport and the use of rented cars at the destination. This will greatly expand markets for car rental firms, and their volume will increase by over 20 % per year, to over $2 billion by 1980.

The road construction program's effect will result in more private vehicles using the network for shorter journeys; it will also encourage increased usage of buses. This will have a detrimental effect on short trips taken both on the railways and on internal airlines. For longer journeys and for long distance holiday traffic, however, rail and air transport will continue to grow.

Freight

In many European nations, much freight transportation has moved from the railways and inland waterways. This has resulted in heavier truck traffic, and since the motorways and national roads are not expected to be able to meet the increased traffic needs of the 1970s, most European governments, particularly those in countries in which traffic is heavily congested, are attempting to force freight off the more crowded systems back onto the rail or inland waterways networks. In Germany, for example, restrictions in the form of very high taxes are placed on freighting by trucks on the roads. It is also forbidden for heavy road transport to use the autobahns on weekends. In the U.K., the government's intention is to force long-haul freight transport onto the railways and off the congested road network. In both countries these moves by the government have not been in operating long enough to assess their real effectiveness. But increased pressures will be put on heavy road vehicles to keep them off roads in both urban and semiurban areas.

Übersetzung auf Seite 137

Vocabulary

adequate ('ædıkwıt)	sufficient
annual	of one year, yearly
by-pass n.	road which goes round a town not through it
congested (kən'dʒestid)	overcrowded

destination n.	place to which sb. or sth. is being sent or going to
detrimental	harmful
EEC	EWG, jetzt: EG (auch: Gemeinsamer Markt)
EFTA	European Free Trade Association
encourage v.	promote, stimulate
improvement n. (from: improve v.)	make better
mileage n. ('maılıdʒ)	miles travelled
network n.	complex system
package tour	a holiday organised by a travel bureau
primarily	above all
provide v.	give, supply
rely on (upon) v.	depend, trust
treble v.	make or become three times as much (or many)
trunk road	main road

Questions on the text

1. In which sector of road construction had most been accomplished at the time this article was written?
2. What does the report forecast for the construction of motorways in Western Europe from 1967 to 1980?
3. Which means of transportation will mainly be used by businessmen?
4. This will contribute considerably to expand the market of one branch. Which one?
5. Are there any other statements made on passenger traffic?
6. Which four means of transportation are mentioned?
7. Can you describe the general development of freight transportation as far as mentioned in the report?
8. This development has caused some restrictions in freight transportation in Germany. Can you say which?

Points for discussion

1. Compare the density of road traffic in Great Britain and other European countries.
2. Discuss the pros and cons of imposing a toll for using the motorway network.
3. In your opinion, what should a plan for the rationalization of rail, road, and air traffic imply?
4. Which measures would you propose to subsidise at least partially the public transport deficit?
5. Building more and more urban roads and motorways has a detrimental effect on the environment. How could the environmental impact (noise, visual intrusion, delays to pedestrians etc.) be diminished?

Common transport policy

A year ago, in one of their first fine flourishes in defence of the environment, the Government refused to allow an increase in lorry weights from 32 to 44 tons. It now appears likely that they will have to eat their words, because Europe is proposing a 42-ton maximum, and when Britain joins she must conform to Europe's rules.

For the same reason the Bill placing restrictions on European lorries visiting Britain, currently passing through Parliament, is unlikely to be effective for very long. From this it might appear to some, and particularly to residents of Eastern England fuming at the enormity of foreign vehicles blundering through ancient market towns, the transport implications of Britain's entry into Europe may appear a disaster, at least in environmental terms. In fact this need not be so: it depends very much on the success of negotiations now going on between Britain and the Six over various aspects of transport policy.

Environmental aspects, surprisingly enough, are possibly the least of the worries. Dimensional limits proposed by Europe are in general no more generous than already applies here: less so in the case of lorry height where Britain currently has no limit. Greater lorry weights are proposed, it is true; but there has never been any evidence that a 44-tonner need be more offensive than a 32-tonner. The real argument should be about axle weights, not lorry weights (for it is that damages the road) and about stricter and more effectively enforced controls over the actual causes of nuisance—noise, fumes, etc.—whatever the size and weight of lorry causing it.

It can then be left to local traffic regulation, such as already applies in the City of London and elsewhere, to see that different sizes of lorry are restricted to suitable routes. In the establishment of environmental controls over traffic, it would not be fair to say Europe lags behind Britain, and that entry would therefore drag

Britain back. The fact is that in both Britain and Europe it has been a neglected area; but the neglect is now recognized, and Britain has an important part to play in securing appropriate European action.

It is in the area of transport policy, economics, and commercial regulation, that the real gap lies between Britain and Europe, and it is here that there is a real danger of Britain being dragged back if her negotiators fail to lead Europe forward. In the 1968 Transport Act and other measures, Britain has a transport policy well ahead of Europe's and indeed of the world's. It gives both road and rail transport a commercial freedom unequalled elsewhere and in social grants to buses and trains provides a better basis than others enjoy for recognizing and maximizing (though the machinery is far from perfect yet) the separate social and commercial benefits of the transport system.

In Europe both road and rail transport still suffer from an army of bureaucrats and a vast body of regulations designed to restrict competition and commercial freedom, and it is inconceivable—it would certainly be extremely costly—that Britain should return to such a world after three bracing years of fruitful evolution. Fortunately there are those in Europe who recognize the need to throw off these shackles and move forward to a more dynamic and enlightened transport policy. To help them to do so should be one of Britain's most important early contributions to the community.

Übersetzung auf Seite 139

Vocabulary

axle n.	Achse
blundering	driving noisily
bracing	refreshing invigorating
conform to v.	comply with, obey, keep to, observe
currently	at the moment, at present, now
disaster n.	catastrophe
drag back v.	hold back, throw back
eat one's words	take back one's words

enforce v.	here: apply
enlightened	progressive
environment n.	surroundings
evidence n.	proof
flourish n. ('flʌrıʃ)	here: gesture, display of action
fume v.	be very angry
implication n.	here: by-product; Begleiterscheinung
inconceivable	unthinkable, unimaginable
lag behind v.	be behind, be less progressive than
neglect v.	ignore, disregard
offensive	unattractive, unacceptable
shackles (pl.) n.	chains, fetters, restraint
social grant	subsidy
unequalled	not achieved elsewhere, without comparison, unique

Questions on the text

1. Why does it seem that the British Government will have to allow an increase in lorry weights?
2. Why might the inhabitants of Eastern England be dissatisfied with the transport implications of Britain's entry into Europe?
3. According to the article, why should more consideration be given to axle weights than to lorry weights?
4. In which fields is Britain more advanced than the rest of Europe?
5. What is the essence of Britain's transport policy?
6. What are the author's reasons for suggesting that Europe should adopt a more progressive transport policy?

Points for discussion

1. Environmental control has been neglected until recently. Why?
2. Would you support the view that a government should impose restrictive measures to control economic development (e.g. wage and price freezes, nationalisation of industries, control of land speculation)? Give reasons for your answer.
3. Discuss the benefits of a coordinated transport policy and say how far you think this has been achieved in Europe.

Trouble again with monster lorries

It is time to be anxious again about monster lorries. Last Thursday the Commons gave the third and final reading to the Government's Bill which gives power to inspect juggernauts from the Continent on arrival and turn them back if they do not comply with British regulations on weight, size and safety. This coming month, the Council of Minister of the European Community has on its agenda proposals from the European Commission which, if they were effected, would overthrow these same British standards when we enter the Common Market.

The proposals for increased weight and size, which are now before the Community, are already the subject of heated argument among its existing members. The British Government is showing itself fairly firm in resisting the new heavy weight proposed—but by no means firm enough. For whereas a month or two back, Ministers were still making noises to indicate that entering the Common Market would not mean raising the British weight limit, the Government has now reached the conclusion that some increase in the permitted weight of juggernauts is unavoidable. What it is doing is digging its heels in against accepting the Commission's full proposals.

In this it has allies among the Six, notably Germany but also Holland, and it is presumed that the other new applicants will be on the same side. In the end, the juggernaut rules will be decided in a tug-of-war between these countries and France which, as always, is proving obdurate and rigid in defence of what she regards as her national interest.

The essential dispute is over weight rather than size. The axle weight of $11\frac{1}{2}$ tons and the gross weight of 42 tons proposed by the EEC is wholly unacceptable to Britain, which limits gross weight to 32 tons and axle weight to 10 tons. For damage to the roads, it is the axle weight which matters. Holland, Germany and Italy are also on 10 tons, though only the first two seem to be particularly keen to keep it there.

To strengthen the whole British road system to take the weights proposed by the Commission would cost £300 million and £10 million a year on new roads, quite apart from the fearful environmental cost. Yet the British Government seems prepared to accept some gross weight increase up to less than 40 tons. What is more, the Government apparently has no objection to increasing the length from the present 15 metres in Britain to 15½—the argument here being that half a metre more on vehicles of this size is neither here nor there. But it is. The size of these vehicles is already too great for a civilised environment.

Whatever happens, Britain should be more rigid in excluding juggernauts from towns and country roads. What is needed is a strictly defined heavy goods network based on the motorways, with special access roads and garage-warehouses which could be the working bases for the heavier lorries.

And, of course, there should be a determination to develop our railways, one of the finest but most undervalued of our capital assets.

Übersetzung auf Seite 141

Vocabulary

allies (pl.) n.	Alliierte, Verbündete
axle n.	Achse
capital assets (pl.)	Anlagevermögen
determination n.	firm intention
dig one's heels in	stand firm
environment n.	surroundings
(environmental adj. from environment)	
juggernaut n.	nightmare, bugbear, menace, giant
obdurate	obstinate, stubborn
presume v.	assume, expect, anticipate
resist v.	stand firm against, refuse, reject
rigid	inflexible
tug-of-war n.	Tauziehen

warehouse n.   store, building where goods are stored

Questions on the text

1. What is the aim of the Bill mentioned at the beginning of the article?
2. Which particular features of lorries are the subject of controversy here?
3. How has the British Government's attitude on this matter changed?
4. Which are the opposing parties in the question of the transport regulations?
5. Why isn't it feasible for Britain to adopt the proposals of the European Commission?
6. What does the author of the article suggest could be done to keep juggernauts out of the towns and off the smaller roads?

Points for discussion

1. Discuss the comparative advantages and disadvantages of road and rail transport.
2. In how far, do you think, individual countries should sacrifice their national interests for the sake of the Community? Give reasons for your answer.
3. If you were Minister of Transport, how would you reconcile the shortage of money and land for road construction and the pollution of the atmosphere with the interests of the car industry?
4. The above article examines the difficulties of reaching agreement on a common transport policy. Name other fields where the Community is aiming at coordination among its members.

Clean-Air Buff

Stiff federal controls on carbon monoxide and hydrocarbon emissions, scheduled to take hold on 1975 model cars, have been a migraine for the automakers. But for Milton Rosenthal, a lawyer who is chief executive of Engelhard Minerals & Chemicals Corp., Washington's demand for cleaner air could produce a bonanza. Engelhard makes a catalytic converter—a steel cylinder containing a platinum-treated honeycomb structure—that changes some toxic gases into harmless substances. The converter, which costs less than $50, shows strong evidence of enabling the automakers to meet the Environmental Protection Agency standards.

Various companies are trying to perfect similar devices, but with the 1975 models already on the planning boards, the auto manufacturers must already begin to line up supplies. Ford was the first, recently making a "firm commitment" with Engelhard for half of the catalytic converters it will need in 1975. Other U.S. automakers may soon follow Ford's lead, and Rosenthal, 58, a meticulous executive who tries to keep an eye on details, is looking abroad for still more customers. Japan and Canada, he believes, will soon pass restrictive emission standards.

Engelhard is an unusual company. It was long run by flamboyant Charles Engelhard, who before his death last year built up a billion-dollar business, mostly as an international trader and fabricator of precious metals. Engelhard does much business with Anglo-American Corp. of South Africa Ltd., which owns 30% of Engelhard's common stock and is run by Harry Oppenheimer, the South African mining magnate. But Rosenthal clearly would welcome any new business. Last year, on revenues of $1.5 billion, the company's earnings dropped from $36 million to $28 million.

Übersetzung auf Seite 143

Vocabulary

bonanza n.	boom, fortune
buff n.	here: cleaning
commitment n.	here: contract, definite arrangement
common stock	shares
device n.	apparatus
flamboyant	enthusiastic, extravert, dynamic
honeycomb	wabenartig
line up v.	queue, procure
meticulous	accurate, thorough, careful, exact, precise
precious metals	e.g. gold and silver
revenues (pl.) n.	here: returns, income
stiff	strict, vigorous
take hold on	affect, take effect on
toxic	poisonous

Questions on the text

1. What does the demand for cleaner air mean for the car manufacturers and for Mr. Rosenthal?
2. What is the catalytic converter made by Engelhard Minerals & Chemicals Corp.? And what is it for?
3. Why does Rosenthal think he will find customers abroad?
4. What type of business did the late Charles Engelhard build up?
5. Why would Rosenthal welcome new lines of business?

Points for discussion

1. What functions, in your opinion, has the Environmental Protection Agency?
2. Discuss the interrelations between economic growth and environmental protection.
3. What measures can a government take to improve the quality of life?
4. Do you think that a reduction of fuel supplies would lead to cleaner air? Give reasons for your answer.
5. What chances, in your opinion, will cars driven by electricity have in the future?

A fresh breeze from Stockholm

The claims for the Stockholm conference on the human environment have been pitched high. It has been called a turning point in history. It was to produce in its declaration a new code of international conduct expressing new concepts of sovereignty more fitting in a world which is at last seen to be "only one earth."

Things have not quite worked out like that. Nations continue to behave like nations—badly. The declaration does establish some important new principles of responsibility to the environment but it also reasserts the old claims to national sovereignty and every country's right to exploit its own natural resources.

Still, it would be a mistake to be too cynical about the Stockholm conference. There is a new mood abroad, and it may be that the exchange of ideas between politicians and scientists it has provoked will have important results in the long run. Indeed, there are now a good many leading politicians of a good many countries who are looking at policies of growth and development with a new perspective. But the conference has also shown what a lot of persuasion there is still to do.

Stockholm has been useful in demonstrating that when 114 nations are gathered together the environmentalists are not preaching to the converted—by no means, with France and China sticking to their rights to pollute the atmosphere with nuclear tests, with Latin-American countries jealously guarding their interests in exploiting the great rivers and forests, with Japan putting the interests of whale hunters before the world-wide concern for the survival of the whale, and with China contemptuously rejecting the pessimism of the Malthusians and other brands of exponential alarmists.

So the week-long attempt to find consensus for the declaration broke down on the fact there is no global consensus. The declaration therefore, is a patchwork of concessions to opposing interests and opposite ideas. This is, of course, a fair reflection of the state of the world.

Granted that we have to operate within the politics of rival national self-interest, there is progress to report. The Stockholm conference agreed on an impressive array of international programmes—for example, for global monitoring of the seas and the atmosphere, for surveys of soil, forest, and energy resources, for the protection of the diversity of the World's genetic heritage of plants and living creatures. The international community of scientists, at any rate, is genuinely international in spirit and knows what is needed.

But these are recommendations for action by others, by governments, or regional groups, or United Nations agencies, or by world-wide conventions. So one note of sceptical reserve must be sounded. The Stockholm conference could do nothing but agree on forms of words. If the General Assembly agrees, there will soon be a coordinating and chivying General Council of Environmental Programmes. But the path to action must wind through the labyrinths of the UN bureaucracy and of governments.

Is this the kind of structure that will activate quickly enough the environmental projects that everyone knows are urgent? Suppose a crisis situation begins to develop through the pollution of the seas. Would the bureaucracies move in time? Would they even have enough money to move? The processes of political action can so easily frustrate the best of ideas.

Übersetzung auf Seite 144

Vocabulary

array n. (əˈreɪ)	display, assortment
chivy v. (also: chevy)	chase, worry; hier: anspornen, antreiben
... claims ... have been pitched high	die Ziele ... waren hochgesteckt
conduct n.	behaviour
consensus n.	common agreement
contemptuously	scornfully
environment n.	surroundings

environmentalist n.	expert in environmental matters
forms of words	Formulierungen
fair reflection	getreues Spiegelbild
genetic heritage	genetisches Erbe
General Assembly	Vollversammlung (der UNO)
jealously	possessively, keenly
monitoring	Überwachung
Malthusian (from Malthus, Thomas Robert)	Thomas Robert Malthus, 1766—1834, English economist, cf. Malthusian Theory of Population
patchwork n.	Flickwerk
pollute v.	make dirty
persuasion n. (pə'sweɪʒən)	power of persuading
persuade v.	convince, influence by argument
reassert v.	put forward again
sound a note	einen Ton anschlagen
survival n.	continuing to live
whale hunter	Walfischfänger

Questions on the text

1. What was the Stockholm conference expected to bring about?
2. What was the result of the conference?
3. Did the conference appeal to the nations to give up national sovereignty?
4. Which rights of every country were reasserted?
5. What are France and China blamed for? Why are Japan and the Latin-American countries mentioned here?
6. Why could no consensus for a common declaration be achieved?
7. Can you give some examples of the positive aspects of the conference?
8. To what degree does the Stockholm conference involve the UN?
9. Which main problems still remain unsolved?

Points for discussion

1. Would you consider the Stockholm conference to be a turning point in history?
2. Discuss how economic interests and protection of the environment are linked.
3. Protection of the environment is expensive. Who should bear the costs in your opinion?
4. Do you think the EEC could play an important role in solving the pollution problem?
5. Study the importance of the UN in this respect.

Spaceship earth or mucky rivers?

One of the better sayings of 1971 was Mr. Peter Walker's declaration, made more than once, that the first priority of his department is to improve the quality of the environment. It was rather more than a thumping statement of the obvious, for the setting up of the Department of the Environment by the amalgamation of an assortment of Ministries dealing with local government, planning, housing, and transport seemed a somewhat blatant bit of bandwagonmanship at the time.

Mr. Walker, to his credit, is proving that he is serious about his department's title. His plans for cleaning up rivers, the promise of heavy fines and even imprisonment for polluters, the tougher line taken on the noise and size of road vehicles, and some development decisions, such as the site for the third London airport, have all been symptomatic of welcome new attitudes. The fact that they are now accepted without serious dispute shows how rapidly things have been changing. The human race has been taking the environment for granted for millennia. Awareness of what we have been doing to it has come only in the last decade—or even only in the past few years. From now on, it might be said the environment will always be with us.

Whether the politicians are now managing to catch up with what needs to be done remains in question. Optimists can point to the success of clean air legislation in this country, and to the improvement of some rivers even before Mr. Walker's clean-up programme gets under way.

Not all progress is headed towards catastrophe, as the pessimists would have it. Nevertheless the pessimists are making the running, and moving the argument away from mundane matters of pollution to such global concerns as the exhaustion of metal and fuel supplies within a generation or two. The statistical trends support their case. From there they move on to condemn the worship of growth as the root of all evil. The world does not have the physical resources, it is argued, to sustain anything like the level of wealth now enjoyed by the developed countries for the prospective world population by the end of this century. So the politicians are told they must find some alternative to growth as the mainspring of their economies. It is a tall order, surely, when three quarters of the world's population is poor or very poor.

Yet the dilemma will not go away. It will have to be tackled, if only in a preliminary and exploratory way, during 1972. In June in Stockholm there is to be a United Nations world conference on the human environment. The conference will be most useful if it can stick fairly strictly to the short-term and the practical.

The practical controls of pollution must not be lightly dismissed as trivial tinkering while "spaceship earth" goes down. Doom watching can be a mere emotional indulgence. There is encouraging evidence to show that bad situations can be retrieved; rivers can recover, and the oceans too; developed agriculture could sustain far larger populations; wildlife often shows remarkable resilience and adaptability.

Most of the answers will depend on technology and technical skills, as well as political decision. There is no escape into some de-urbanised, de-motorised, de-schooled utopia. The problem is to stabilise an industrial science-based civilisation. Countermeasures to pollution by themselves will admittedly not be enough. Much larger issues of policy will have to be confronted. The free play of economic greed in the free market is a sure course to disaster, and we shall need a new scale of values which will replace quantity of growth by quality of growth. But that is a theme for a generation rather than for a new year or ten days in Stockholm.

Übersetzung auf Seite 146

Vocabulary

bandwagonmanship n.	hier: Effekthascherei
blatant ('bleɪtənt)	shamelessly obvious
concerns (pl.) n.	interests
department n.	here: ministry

disaster n.	catastrophe
doom watching	pessimistic outlook on the state of the world
environment n.	surroundings
exhaustion n.	drying up, using up completely
fine n.	amount of money paid as punishment for breaking a law or rule
fuel supplies	Brennstoffvorräte
greed n.	selfish desire
improve v.	make better
indulgence n. (from: indulge v.)	satisfaction of desires
mainspring n.	driving or motivating force, vital part
millenia (pl.) n. (singular: millenium)	periods of thousands of years
mundane	here: everyday
mucky	dirty
polluter n.	Umweltverschmutzer
preliminary	here: first
retrieve v.	amend, restore to a flourishing state
resilience n.	ability to resist
spaceship n.	Raumschiff
sustain v.	maintain, here: support
tackle v.	deal with
thumping	forceful

Questions on the text

1. What did Mr. Walker say was the main concern of his department?
2. Which ministries had been amalgamated to form the new Department of the Environment?
3. Are there any concrete plans to improve the quality of the environment? If so, which ones?
4. Why do the pessimists "make the running"?
5. Why do the pessimists condemn the worship of growth as the root of all evil?

6. How will the Stockholm conference be most useful?
7. Which examples of retrieving bad situations are mentioned?
8. What new scale of values will be needed?

Points for discussion

1. Discuss the terms "quantity of growth" and "quality of growth".
2. Do you think that a de-urbanised, de-motorised, and de-schooled world would be a solution to our environmental problems? Give reasons for your answer.
3. State the advantages and disadvantages of the amalgamation of the afore mentioned ministries to form the Department of the Environment.
4. Assuming the statistical forecast on the exhaustion of metal and fuel supplies is right, do you then think that mankind will die out or find other resources in order to survive?
5. If you were Minister for the Environment, what measures would you take to improve the quality of life?
6. "Half of the human race should be exterminated"—would this step, in your opinion, be suitable to solve the problem of the population explosion?

Take a sober look at doomsday

If 10 days is a long time in politics, 10 years is virtually unthinkable. This may turn out to be the crux of what environmentalists are now calling the predicament of mankind. Evidently the world cannot sustain unlimited growth with limited resources—but how many politicians believe that this has anything to do with the politics of this year or next?

The Club of Rome, an international group of scientists, economists, industrialists, civil servants, and academics of substantial reputation, is now trying to convince the world that it is headed for catastrophic collapse within the next 100 years or so if present rates of population increase and economic growth continue. Suddenly, and quite soon, demand for food and natural resources of one kind and another will outrun supply, and some crucial non-renewable resources, such as petroleum and various essential metals, will be exhausted. Economic and social collapse will follow.

Some doomwatch prophecies have been criticised as hysterical. The Club of Rome's report "The Limits to Growth" is a sober, if chilling, technical examination of the likely trends in the next 130 years made by an expert team of computer specialists at the Massachusetts Institute of Technology. No doubt some of the assumptions fed into a complicated computer model will turn out to be wrong. Even so, the MIT case demands the most serious examination. Perhaps its figures are awry—but they must be proved to be so. Perhaps the MIT team are too pessimistic about so far undiscovered resources, or the potential of solar energy as a power supply. Yet they tried assuming unlimited resources, and the answer they got only slowed down the onset of collapse.

The conclusions they reach are essentially two: that births and deaths must be brought into balance; and that capital investment should not exceed capital depreciation (the zero growth argument). Stabilisation must replace growth. But at what level? And when? The developing countries are only beginning to reach towards the affluence others more fortunate already enjoy.

The Club of Rome recognises the moral and political dilemmas in working for a state of global equilibrium. But if the calculations of this report are even approximately right, the cost of political delay could be appalling for this generation of children and their children. Governments cannot say they have not been warned.

The warning could prove to be alarmist, but it would be rash to assume, without contrary evidence, that it will be.

Übersetzung auf Seite 148

Vocabulary

affluence n.	wealth
appalling (ə'pɔlɪŋ)	shocking, terrible, catastrophic
awry (ə'raɪ)	wrong
collapse n.	break down
crux n.	essence
delay n.	postponement, putting off until later
depreciation n.	dropping in value, amortisation
Doomsday n.	the Day of Judgement, the end of the world
economic growth	Wirtschaftswachstum
exhaust v.	use up completely
outrun v.	exceed, surpass
predicament n. (prɪ'dɪkəmənt)	situation from which escape seems difficult or impossible
sober	not drunk, calm; here: realistic
solar energy	Sonnenenergie

Questions on the text

1. Why can unlimited growth not be sustained?
2. What is the Club of Rome?
3. Why do they think mankind will suffer a total collapse within the next 100 years?

4. Who made the report "The Limits to Growth" and what are its main conclusions?
5. What is understood by the "zero growth argument"?
6. Which questions remain unsolved?

Points for discussion

1. Define and discuss the term "quality of life".
2. How can you change your daily habits in order to contribute towards a lower degree of pollution?
3. Do you think that rapid economic growth is at least partly responsible for pollution? Give reasons for your statement.
4. Imagine a world without oil. Try to find out what oil is needed for and which substitutes exist.

World food situation worst for years

The world food situation this year is worse than at any time since the years immediately after the Second World War. Against a constantly rising population, 1973 looks like being the first year since the war that world food production has actually declined.

This is the gloomy analysis published on Monday by the director-general of the United Nations Food and Agriculture Organisation in Rome, Dr. A. H. Boerma. The report was written before the current harvest was in, but Dr. Boerma finds sufficient bad news about 1972 to predict worse consequences this year.

With a world population growth of 2 per cent, food and agricultural production dropped 3 per cent per person, and fishery production fell 1 per cent.

"Cereal stocks have dropped to the lowest level for 20 years," he says. "In the new situation of world-wide shortage, prices are rocketing and the world's biggest agricultural exporter has had to introduce export allocations for certain products (the US restrictions on soya beans)."

"There have now been two successive years of poor harvests in the developing countries. In 1972, the Near East was the only developing region to record a large increase, and a substantial drop in the Far East of about 4 per cent caused a decline of about 1 per cent in the total food production of the developing countries."

Dr. Boerma points out that while in 1971 there was a bumper harvest in the rich countries, last year's drop in the developing countries was complicated by disastrous weather in the Soviet Union, causing shortages among the rich countries.

Because of the massive purchases by the Russians, he says, world stocks of wheat are down to the lowest level for 20 years and rice is also in very short supply.

"There is therefore little if any margin against the possibility of another widespread harvest failure in 1973, and the world has become dangerously dependent on current production, and hence, on the weather."

In fact, harvesting has been near expectations, although there has been some damage in the Soviet Union. But Dr. Boerma points out: "The real measure of our anxiety is that while a marginal shortfall in a major area in 1973 could lead to a serious deficit at the world level, a marginal improvement would not much relieve what is already a dangerous situation."

While grain merchants have been predicting a build-up of stocks next year, Dr. Boerma says that so much depends on the weather that it is too early to form any reliable picture of the outcome, and developing countries are facing special difficulties this year in planting because of shortages and high prices in world fertiliser markets.

Übersetzung auf Seite 150

Vocabulary

actually	in fact
allocation n.	quota
anxiety n. (æn'zaɪətɪ)	worry, concern
bumper	extra large, abundant
cereal n.	grain
disastrous	catastrophic
fertiliser n.	Düngemittel
gloomy	pessimistic
grain n.	e.g. wheat, barby, etc.
hence	therefore, thus
margin n.	here: reserve
marginal	slight, narrow
outcome n.	result
reliable	dependable
relieve v.	aid, help
rocket v.	shoot up
shortfall n.	shortage
substantial	large, considerable
successive	one after the other, consecutive

Questions on the text

1. What is said in the UN analysis of the world food production for 1973?
2. How does the world food production compare with the world population growth?
3. What was the harvest situation in the Near East and the Far East in 1972?
4. What has the Soviet Union caused to buy large quantities of wheat?
5. What would be the consequences of both marginal shortfall and a marginal improvement of harvests in a major production area?
6. Which are the special difficulties of the developing countries?

Points for discussion

1. Agricultural productivity in developing countries is lower than in highly developed countries. Discuss.
2. Farmers tend to prefer poor harvests to rich ones. Why?
3. Discuss the relationships between a food crisis and
   a) agricultural prices
   b) growing populations
4. We are a wasteful society. How can we avoid such waste?

Two significant post-war years

The International Institute for Strategic Studies in its Strategic Survey for 1971 draws a careful comparison between last year and 1947, as, historically, perhaps the two most significant years since the war. Posterity must provide judgment, but the interim reflection is intriguing because their similarity lies in their dissimilarity. In both, the world, having been shaken round like a kaleidoscope finally emerged with a discernibly new pattern. In 1947 what appeared was the shape of the cold war with the Soviet Union and the United States thrown into relief. In 1971 the old order, in Asia at least, dramatically changed, as China and Japan, two non-white nations, advanced more clearly into the scene.

The difficulty of inferring very much from last year is that so much that happened during the twelve months belonged more to the future than to the past. Some things were accomplished, notably the successful outcome to the Berlin Talks, the long overdue entry of China to the United Nations, the ascendancy of India in the subcontinent through her victory over Pakistan in the fortnight war before Christmas, and the withdrawal of British forces from Singapore and the Persian Gulf. But rather more was initiated without anything very firm being accomplished.

The Strategic Arms Limitation Talks (SALT) provided promise of some kind of agreement between America and the Soviet Union this year, one which should concentrate on defensive weapons, with some linkage to offensive weaponry too. Vietnamization advanced in South-East Asia, and the Americans steadily withdrew. Japan nudged China gently in an effort to win friends and influence people in a changing East.

There was certainly, in general, more "jaw-jaw" than "war-war". And happily most of it centred on or around arms control. But not all the talking accomplished as much as might have been hoped. If 1971 was the year in which, as the IISS puts it, a new "great power quadrilateral" developed in East Asia and a new "concert of major powers" worldwide, then what of 1972? The biological weapons treaty promised in 1971 has materialized. But Mr Manlio Brosio, who has been the Nato emissary to Moscow to discuss talks about talks about balanced force reductions still sits in the wings awaiting his cue from Mr. Brezhnev. The German political crisis has threatened to defer Ostpolitik, and any complacency which may ever have been felt about Vietnam has proved quite unreal.

But the most constant element this year, last year and in the years immediately preceding it, must be the growth in power and influence of the Chinese, despite their setback in the Indo-Pakistan War when they backed the losing side and failed to prop it up. The growth of Soviet forces deployed in the military districts along that 7,000-mile frontier only emphasizes the point.

The trebling of these forces in the past three years is clearly meant, says the Survey, to "deter or dominate" the kind of armed incidents which happened on the Ussuri River in 1969—and the Russian preference must be for "deterrence." Militarily China remains in a league behind the superpowers with the development of an intercontinental ballistic missile of the 4,000-mile range class still probably several years away.

But diplomatically China has pushed herself or rather eased herself into the first division, and in the eastern hemisphere has become a force whom the two superpowers will never be able to discount again. This emergence, coupled with that of Japan is what really characterized 1971. Perhaps not even 1947 contained anything quite as significant.

Übersetzung auf Seite 152

Vocabulary

accomplish v.	achieve, finish successfully
armed incidents	bewaffnete Zwischenfälle
ascendancy n.	rising in importance
back v.	support
balanced force reduction	ausgewogene Truppen-reduzierung

complacency n.	self-satisfaction
defer v.	postpone, put off until later
deploy v.	position
deter v.	discourage
deterrence n.	attempt to prevent or stop sth.
discernible	(sth. that) can be seen clearly
discount v.	ignore, disregard, overlook
emissary n.	representative, person sent to deliver a message
gentle	mild
infer	imply, suggest
interim	intermediate
intrigue v.	arouse the interest or curiosity
jaw-jaw n.	talks, discussion
linkage n.	inclusion
materialize v.	become fact
nudge v.	push gently with the elbow
outcome n.	result
posterity n.	future generations
prop up v.	support physically
quadrilateral n.	four-sided figure
range n.	here: effective distance
SALT (Strategic Arms Limitation Talks)	Gespräche über eine strategische Rüstungsbegrenzung
shape n.	outer form, pattern
survey n.	examination, study
treble v.	make three times greater
war-war n.	hier: Kriegsgeschrei, Säbelrasseln
weaponry, weapons n.	arms; Waffen
(biological weapons)	(bakteriologische Waffen)
withdrawal n.	removal

Questions on the text

1. Why does the IISS-survey choose specifically the years 1947 and 1971 for a comparison?
2. What do these years have in common?
3. In which way did the old order in the world change?

4. Which events worth mentioning and referred to in the text took place in 1971?
5. Which kinds of weapons do SALT include?
6. Why did Japan approach China?
7. What does the trebling of Soviet forces along the Russian-Chinese frontier mean?
8. Why does the author think China will remain behind the superpowers for some years to come?
9. What is characteristic of the year 1971?

Points for discussion

1. How would you judge the efforts of SALT?
2. Would you consider MBFR (Mutual Balanced Force Reduction) as an adequate means for making our world safer?
3. What efforts, in your opinion, should be made by a peace research programme?
4. Young people throughout the world demand more money to be spent on education and less on armaments. Do you think that conflicts among nations could be solved on this basis? Give examples of military conflicts and try to find plans to solve them peacefully.

ARMS CONTROL
Agreement on Enough

The White House last week announced a "major advance" in the Strategic Arms Limitation Talks, which have been going on since 1969. The advance—a compromise worked out in a secret exchange of letters between President Nixon and Soviet Party Chief Leonid Brezhnev—represents an important milestone in U.S.-Soviet relations and reflects a long-term change in Washington's policy. Where once the U.S. sought to maintain overall nuclear superiority, Washington has now settled for what Nixon has called "sufficiency"—that is, enough arms to deter any Russian attack by promising a devastating retaliatory strike.

Though many difficult details must still be worked out by SALT negotiators, now meeting in Helsinki, the overall shape of the nuclear accommodation between the superpowers was beginning to emerge. The U.S. and the Soviet Union agreed to a series of ceilings and freezes in which Washington has consented to Soviet parity—and in several cases numerical superiority—in every major category of defensive and offensive strategic nuclear weaponry. In return, the Soviets made two important concessions.

They agreed to place limits on the numbers of missile subs. But more important, they agreed to exclude from the present freeze U.S. tactical nuclear weapons in Europe and aboard the Sixth Fleet in the Mediterranean. Hence the U.S. was able to avoid unnerving its European NATO allies, who would look askance at any unilateral dealing with the Soviets over American weaponry that is committed to the defense of Western Europe.

The compromise virtually ensures that Nixon and Brezhnev will be able to have a historic signing ceremony if and when the President visits Moscow later this month. They will probably have two documents to sign. One is a full-fledged treaty, already agreed upon, limiting the number of defensive ABMs, or anti-ballistic missiles, that each side may install. The second, barring any last-minute snag, will be an executive agreement setting informal ceilings on offensive strategic missiles until the SALT negotiators can come up with a formal pact. The major points of the two documents:

ABMS. The U.S. and the Soviet Union will each be permitted to maintain only two ABM complexes of 100 missiles each. The Soviets, who have chosen to defend populated areas, will probably add new missiles to the 64 ABMs that now ring Moscow. They may also convert the Tallin Line of antiaircraft missiles near Leningrad to ABMs. The U.S., which by contrast has chosen to use the alloted ABMs to protect its land-based missile force, originally had announced its intention to build 14 Safeguard ABM complexes. Now it will complete only the two sites at Grand Forks. N. Dak., and Malmstrom, Mont.

ICMBS. Pending a formal treaty, both superpowers will freeze the number of ICBMs at the present level, which leaves the U.S. at a 2-to-3 disadvantage (1,054 v. 1,550). Both sides will be free to replace older missiles with newer ones. More important, no ceiling has been placed on nuclear megatonnage, a category in which the Soviets already have far outdistanced the U.S. and which helps them overcome their disadvantage of having less accurate missiles. In fact, some Pentagon experts expect the Russians to install new monster ICBMs in the big empty silos that have recently been detected by U.S. surveillance satellites. The U.S. has more warheads on its missiles—5,700 to the Soviets' 2,500, though Moscow will be allowed to draw even on that score. At present, the U.S. has a considerable technological lead. Its MIRV (multiple independently targeted re-entry vehicle) warheads can be steered to widely separated targets. By comparison, the Russian MRVs (multiple re-entry vehicles) simply fall in a prearranged cluster.

MISSILE SUBS. Unter the ceiling, the Soviets, who have lagged far behind the U.S. in the development of undersea nuclear missiles, will be permitted to complete the 17 submarines now abuilding; within the next couple of years Moscow's missile-packing submarine force will outnumber by one the 41-ship U.S. undersea missile fleet.

Even though the compromise on offensive weapons allows for technological improvement—the U.S., for instance, may eventually replace its missile submarines with the undersea long-range missile system (ULMS), at $165 million per sub without armament —it nevertheless promises to bring the nuclear numbers race to a halt. It also, it is hoped, will serve as a guideline for a full-fledged treaty that will regulate offensive missiles in the same manner in which the ABMs have been brought under control. When, and if, that happens, the strategic arms pact will rank historically with the nuclear test-ban treaty (1963) and the nuclear nonproliferation treaty (1968).

Übersetzung auf Seite 154

Vocabulary

accommodation n.	here: arrangement
allot v.	distribute, assign
allow for v.	take into consideration
anti-aircraft missiles	Flugabwehrraketen (Luft-Luft, Boden-Luft)
anti-ballistic missiles (ABMs)	Anti-Raketen Raketen
barring	here: without
ceiling n.	maximum level
cluster n.	small group of objects
deter v.	abschrecken
devastate v.	ruin
emerge v.	appear
ensure v.	make sure or certain
full-fledged	hier: ausgereift
ICBM (intercontinental ballistic missile)	Interkontinentalrakete
install v.	place
look askance at	look at with suspicion, be suspicious of
missile n. ('mɪsaɪl) am. ('mɪsɪl)	Rakete
missile sub. (missile submarine)	raketenbewaffnetes U-Boot

99

multiple independently targeted re-entry vehicles (MIRV)	Weltraumrakete mit Vielfachsprengkörper (Bombenträger, die im Orbit bis auf Abruf kreisen)
multiple re-entry vehicles (MRVs)	Weltraumraketen
nuclear megatonnage	atomare Sprengkraft (Megatonnen)
nuclear subs	atomgetriebene Unterseeboote
nuclear nonproliferation treaty	Vertrag über atomare Lieferungsbegrenzungen an Drittländer
nuclear test-ban treaty	Atomtest-Stoppvertrag
outnumber v.	zahlenmäßig überlegen sein
retaliatory	returning ill-treatment for ill-treatment
SALT (Strategic Arms Limitation Talks)	Gespräche über eine strategische Rüstungsbegrenzung
settle v.	hier: sich entschließen zu
snag n.	hidden unknown or unexpected difficulty or obstacle
steer v.	direct the course of
sub n.	abbreviation of "submarine"
surveillance n.	close observation
surveillance satellites	Aufklärungssatelliten
tactical nuclear weapons	taktische Atomwaffen
undersea long-range missile system (ULMS)	Unterwasser-Langstreckenraketensystem
undersea nuclear missile	Unterwasserrakete
warhead n.	Sprengkopf

Questions on the text

1. What compromise was worked out between Nixon and Brezhnev?
2. What is meant when Nixon talks about "Sufficiency"?
3. The U.S. has made an important concession to the Soviet Union. What have the Soviets given in return?
4. Why is it a special problem to the U.S.A. to deal with the Soviets over American weaponry in Western Europe?

5. Can you explain the abbreviations of ABM, ICBM, MIRV and ULM?
6. What will the Soviet Union use the ABMs for?
7. What will the U.S.A. use them for?
8. How can the Soviets overcome the disadvantage of having less accurate missiles than the U.S.A.?
9. What is the difference between the American MIRV and the Russian MRV, as stated in the text?
10. Will the U.S.A. be able to maintain its superiority in the development of undersea nuclear missiles?
11. Is there any chance to bring the nuclear numbers race to a halt? If so, how?

Points for discussion

1. What is the difference between the nuclear test-ban treaty and the nuclear non-proliferation treaty?
2. Would you say that such pacts and treaties really help to achieve detente? Do you see a better way of getting there?
3. Do you think that the United Nations could or should do more in the arms control field? Try to make suggestions.

Consumer Income and Spending

Verbrauchereinkommen und Verbraucherausgaben

Steigende Bevölkerungszahlen und steigende Einkommen werden in den nächsten zwei Jahrzehnten zu einem beträchtlichen Anwachsen der Verbrauchsnachfrage beitragen. In diesem Zeitraum werden sich die realen privaten Verbrauchsausgaben ähnlich wie das Bruttosozialprodukt noch mehr als verdoppeln. Da die Leistungserstellung der Volkswirtschaft wesentlich schneller als die Bevölkerung wächst, wird ebenfalls eine ständige Erhöhung des realen pro-Kopf-Verbrauchs zu verzeichnen sein. Gegenwärtig gibt jeder Amerikaner durchschnittlich etwa 3 300 Dollar jährlich aus; diese Größe steigt, gerechnet auf der heutigen Preisbasis, bis 1990 auf nahezu 6 000 Dollar an. Diese erwartete Verbesserung des Lebensstandards wird sich schneller als in den vorausgegangenen Jahrzehnten vollziehen, vor allem deswegen, weil in den kommenden Jahren der Anteil der arbeitenden Bevölkerung steigt.

Wir erleben in der Tat eine bedeutsame Umverteilung des realen Einkommens; Jahr für Jahr steigen Millionen Familien in der Einkommensskala auf. Dieser Umverteilungsprozeß bestand in der Vergangenheit hauptsächlich in einer Verlagerung des Einkommenniveaus weg vom Existenzminimum. In den kommenden Jahrzehnten wird jedoch ein Großteil der amerikanischen Familien über die Mittel verfügen, um die Produkte und Dienstleistungen bezahlen zu können, die allgemein mit Wohlstand in Verbindung gebracht werden. Gegenwärtig verfügen etwa 12 Mio. Familien, das ist weniger als ein Viertel, über ein Jahreseinkommen von mehr als 15 000 Dollar; in zwanzig Jahren wird diese Gruppe die überwiegende Mehrheit bilden.

Im Jahr 1990 wird es gut 40 Mio. Familien, das sind fast 60 %, mit einem Einkommen über 15 000 Dollar (auf Preisbasis 1971) geben. Ungefähr jede vierte Familie wird 1990 über ein Jahreseinkommen von mehr als 25 000 Dollar verfügen; die Vergleichszahl beträgt heute 1 zu 20.

Dieser Anstieg wird die Armut jedoch nicht gänzlich beseitigen. Obgleich die Armut zurückgeht, wird ihre Existenz ein noch größeres soziales Problem darstellen, eben weil aufgrund der volkswirtschaftlichen Situation zunehmend die Möglichkeit gegeben sein wird, dieses Problem zu mildern. 4,5 Millionen Familien verfügen heutzutage zum Beispiel über ein Jahreseinkommen von weniger als 3 000 Dollar; 1990 wird es noch etwa 2,5 Millionen Familien mit einem Einkommen von weniger als 3 000 Dollar (auf Preisbasis 1971) geben. Diese Angaben basieren jedoch ausschließlich auf statistischen Berechnungen, die mögliche Sozialprogramme in den kommenden Jahren nicht berücksichtigen.

Wenn eine Familie eine höhere Stufe in der Einkommenskala erreicht, wird jeder Dollar dieses zusätzlichen Einkommens verschieden ausgegeben — der Anteil der Ausgaben für Grundbedürfnisse geht gegenüber den sonstigen Ausgaben relativ zurück. Die Ausgaben für Nahrungsmittel und Schuhe stiegen zum Beispiel von 1955 bis 1970 um durchschnittlich etwa 2,5 %/o jährlich, im Vergleich dazu stiegen die Ausgaben für Auslandsreisen und Hochschulausbildung im Durchschnitt um mehr als 6 %/o. Nach wie vor werden einige Bereiche des Konsumgütersektors schneller als andere wachsen. Das Verhalten der Verbraucher bei steigender Kaufkraft in jüngster Vergangenheit deutet zumindest an, was für die vor uns liegende Zeit zu erwarten sein dürfte.

THE POOR Getting poorer and poorer

Die Armen werden immer ärmer

Ausgerechnet am letzten Tag der Sondierungsgespräche zwischen der Regierung und dem TUC[1]) über Stufe III[2]) wurde neues Material veröffentlicht, aus dem ersichtlich ist, wie es den Reichen immer besser und den Armen immer schlechter geht, seit die konservative Regierung im Amt ist. Diese Angaben, die auf den Einkommen nach Steuer basieren und der Statistik über Familienausgaben für 1972 entnommen sind, müssen erst noch von den Politikern „geschluckt" werden. Sie könnten zu einer völlig neuen Politik führen und die Grundlage einer zukünftigen Einkommenspolitik, sei es unter dieser oder einer anderen Regierung, bilden.

In der Statistik über Familienausgaben werden die neuesten Angaben über die Einkommensverteilung und die ersten Aussagen über das Jahr 1972 gemacht. Damit kann man zum ersten Mal Rückschlüsse aus dem, wenn auch relativ kurzfristigen, Einfluß der konservativen Regierung auf die Verteilung der nach Steuerabzug verfügbaren Löhne und Gehälter ziehen. Die Lehren für die gegenwärtige Wirtschaftspolitik sind überaus wichtig und dürfen nicht länger ignoriert werden.

Wenn man die Daten über die Verteilung des Brutto- und Nettoeinkommens aufbereitet und zu den Angaben in der amtlichen Steuerstatistik für 1970 in Beziehung setzt, wird ein Vergleich mit den Tabellen über die Einkommensverteilung in der offiziellen Landesstatistik bis 1967 ermöglicht (danach wurden diese Tabellen leider nicht mehr veröffentlicht). Die sich daraus ergebende Aussage ist weit entfernt von dem Mythos eines stumpfer werdenden Gleichheitskegels, wie er so gern von vielen Konservativen verbreitet wird.

[1]) TUC = Trades Union Congress, der Dachverband der britischen Gewerkschaften — Anm. d. Übers.

[2]) Stufe III des Stabilitätsprogramms der britischen Regierung — Anm. d. Übers.

Es stimmt schon, daß die reichen 10 % der Bevölkerung in den letzten 25 Jahren Einbußen im Einkommensanteil hinnehmen mußten, welcher 1949 das gut 2¹/₂fache ihres prozentualen Anteils an der Gesamtbevölkerung betrug und dann etappenweise unter das 2¹/₂-fache fiel. Die große Mittelgruppe mit drei Fünfteln der Bevölkerung konnte ihr Einkommen fortlaufend, wenn auch mit unterschiedlichen Steigerungsraten, erhöhen. 1949 lag ihr Einkommensanteil leicht unter ihrem prozentualen Bevölkerungsanteil. 1972 leicht darüber. Das ärmste Drittel der Bevölkerung hatte zunächst einen Anteil am Gesamteinkommen, der noch nicht einmal der Hälfte seines proportionalen Bevölkerungsanteils entsprach, und die Tendenz geht deutlich zur Verschlechterung seiner Lage.

Wenn ich weiter oben davon ausging, daß die Angaben der Tabelle den Grad der Umverteilung des Einkommens nach Steuerabzug unter der jetzigen konservativen Regierung zeigen, so ist das irreführend, denn die Zahlen für die Zeit von 1970 bis 1972 beschönigen die wahre Situation. Zum einen sind die gestiegenen Beiträge für Schulspeisung, Arztrezepte und andere medizinische Leistungen sowie die erhöhten Mieten für Sozialwohnungen (die natürlich alle aus dem Einkommen nach Steuerabzug bezahlt werden) nicht berücksichtigt; zum anderen ist der Anteil am Einkommen nach Steuerabzug an der Spitze der Skala, d. h. bei den reichsten 10 %, stärker gestiegen als die Tabelle ausweist.

Mit anderen Worten, die 22,0 % in der letzten Spalte sind zu niedrig angesetzt. Das liegt einerseits daran, daß die Rücklaufquote bei den für die Statistik über Familienausgaben Befragten unter den Gutsituierten relativ gering ist, zum zweiten daran, daß die Einkünfte aus Kapitalvermögen für die Statistik über Familienausgaben meistens niedriger angegeben werden als in den Steuererklärungen und zum dritten ergibt sich eine geringfügige Verzerrung durch die Aufbereitung der Daten aus technischen Gründen. Das heißt also, daß die reichsten 10 % der Einkommensempfänger ihren Anteil am Gesamteinkommen nach Steuerabzug deutlich erhöhen konnten. Im Gegensatz zu der allgemein akzeptierten Meinung haben Propaganda und Maßnahmen der gegenwärtigen Regierung also doch einen erheblichen Einfluß auf die Einkommensverteilung zwischen den Bessersituierten und den Armen ausgeübt.

Auch die mittleren Einkommensgruppen konnten ihren Anteil am Einkommen nach Steuerabzug erhöhen — mit anderen Worten nicht nur die obere, sondern auch die mittlere Gruppe bereicherte sich auf Kosten der ärmsten 30 %. Da das Finanzamt Personen mit einem Jahreseinkommen von weniger als 275 Pfund überhaupt nicht veranlagt, könnte der für 1970 mit 14,7 % angegebene Einkommensanteil der ärmsten 30 % etwas zu hoch sein und somit zu einem falschen Eindruck für die Zeit von 1970 bis 1972 führen.

Selbst wenn man dies alles berücksichtigt, ist der Trend eindeutig und politisch konsequent. Fast während der gesamten Nachkriegszeit befanden sich die reichsten 10 % in einer ständig abbröckelnden Einkommenssituation, aber unter der Macmillan-Regierung Anfang der 60er Jahre trat eine zeitweilige Verbesserung ein.

Unter der Wilson-Regierung setzte sich die rückläufige Entwicklung des Einkommensanteils dieser Gruppe fort, um dann seit 1970, dem Amtsantritt der jetzigen Regierung, (stärker als es die Zahlen zeigen) wieder in umgekehrter Richtung zu verlaufen. Bei den Armen dagegen zeigt sich deutlich, daß (trotz der Korrekturen, die man bei den Zahlen machen muß) sich ihr Anteil jeweils umgekehrt proportional zu dem der Reichen bewegt hat.

Der Grund für die jüngsten Veränderungen, wie sie die Tabelle zeigt, war die beträchtliche Senkung der Steuersätze in den Staatshaushalten 1971 und 1972, die sich besonders stark bei dem reichsten Zehntel der Bevölkerung ausgewirkt hat und verhinderte, daß der Rückgang des Bruttoeinkommens zu einem Rückgang auch des Nettoeinkommens führte. Während von 1970 bis 1972 das Einkommen der reichsten 10 % vor Steuer tatsächlich gefallen ist, ist ihr Einkommen nach Steuerabzug in diesem Zeitabschnitt um mindestens 0,5 % gestiegen.

Vor diesem Hintergrund kann Heath die Tatsache, daß sich der Anteil der Armen rückläufig entwickelt und diese Entwicklung korrigiert werden muß, als stärksten Trumpf in Einkommensdiskussionen verwenden. Ein Weg dorthin wäre die Abschaffung wenigstens der gröbsten Ungerechtigkeiten im Dschungel der im Laufe der Zeit planlos entstandenen Steuererleichterungen und -vergünstigungen, und die Verwendung dieser Mehreinnahmen für eine spürbare Erhöhung der Renten und Sozialhilfen für die abhängigen Gruppen sowie zur Anhebung des steuerlichen Grundfreibetrages für die Bezieher niedriger Einkommen.

Großzügige Steuervergünstigungen, deren Wert proportional zum Einkommen wächst, setzen praktisch die Progressivwirkung unserer Ergänzungsabgabe, der sogenannten „Strafsteuer", in den höheren Einkommensbereichen außer Kraft. In Verbindung mit der prozentualen Staffelung des Steuertarifs je nach Bruttoeinkommen ist diese Tatsache die eigentliche Ursache für die bemerkenswerte Widerstandsfähigkeit der Einkommensungleichheit in unserer Gesellschaft.

Durch die Ausschöpfung der Steuervergünstigungen werden sowohl der jeweils höchste Steuersatz (bei 20 000 Pfund Jahreseinkommen z. B. 75 %) als auch der auf das Gesamteinkommen umgerechnete effektive Steuersatz (bei 20 000 Pfund weniger als 50 %) erheblich reduziert.

Nach den von der Regierung jetzt veröffentlichen Angaben hatten diese Steuererleichterungen 1972 für die Begünstigten einen Gesamtwert von etwa 2,5 Mrd. Pfund, die zum größten Teil (wenn auch nicht ausschließlich) den 10 % an der Spitze der Einkommensskala zugute kamen. Diese Steuervergünstigungen setzten sich wie folgt zusammen: Anrechnung der Arbeitnehmeranteile (170 Mio. Pfund) und der Arbeitgeberanteile (650 Mio. Pfund) an den Rentenversicherungsbeiträgen, Ermäßigung für Lebensversicherungsbeiträge (315 Mio. Pfund), für Hypothekenzinsen (390 Mio. Pfund), für Schuldzinsen (7 Mio. Pfund) und Kinderfreibeträge (930 Mio. Pfund). Insgesamt betrugen diese Steuererleichterungen und -vergünstigungen für 1972 nicht weniger als 37 % des gesamten Einkommensteueraufkommens plus Ergänzungsabgabe für hohe Einkommen.

Die Daten der amtlichen Steuerstatistik für 1971 (Tabelle 105) machen deutlich, daß die Steuererleichterungen die Wirkung des angeblich progressiven Einkommensteuertarifs untergraben und eine fiskalische Umverteilung verhindern. Sie zeigen z. B., daß die Steuerermäßigung für Lebensversicherungsbeiträge bei einem Jahreseinkommen von mehr als 10 000 Pfund mindestens 23mal so viel wert ist wie bei einem Jahreseinkommen von weniger als 1 000 Pfund.

Wenn die Steuervergünstigungen für die oberen Einkommensgruppen progressiv reduziert würden, so daß sich der Einnahmeausfall des

Staates um etwa ¹/₃ vermindert, könnten diese zusätzlichen Mittel zur Erhöhung der Altersrente um wöchentlich 2 Pfund und des Kindergeldes um 50 Pence pro Woche benutzt werden, was besonders den niedrig bezahlten Arbeitern zugute käme.

Eine solche Lösung könnte „mit einem Schlag" größere Steuergerechtigkeit und eine gerechtere Einkommensverteilung herbeiführen. Eine Einkommensteuerstruktur, die sich progressiv nennt, hat wenig Sinn, wenn sie Steuererleichterungen gestattet, deren Auswirkung höchst regressiv ist.

Growth Potential of the U.S. Economy

Das Wachstumspotential der amerikanischen Wirtschaft

Die Gesamtleistung der amerikanischen Wirtschaft hat sich in den vergangenen 20 Jahren real mehr als verdoppelt. Zur Zeit werden Waren und Dienstleistungen jährlich für mehr als 1 Billion Dollar erstellt. Unter der Voraussetzung einer Vollbeschäftigung soll das nationale Bruttosozialprodukt bis 1990 insgesamt, auf Preisbasis 1971, mehr als 2,4 Billionen Dollar erreichen.

Konjunktur-, sowie kriegs- und inflationsbedingte Beschäftigungsschwankungen haben zu einer jährlich stark wechselnden Wachstumsrate des BSP geführt. Das Wirtschaftswachstum hat aber auch in Zeiten ähnlicher konjunktureller Verläufe beträchtlichen Schwankungen unterlegen. Unter Zugrundelegung der jeweiligen Konjunkturspitzen war die Wachstumsrate in den Jahren 1948 bis 1953 zum Beispiel mehr als doppelt so hoch wie von 1957 bis 1960.

Bei unseren Vorausberechnungen gehen wir davon aus, daß die Wirtschaft in den nächsten 20 Jahren konjunkturellen Schwankungen unterliegt; der vorgegebene Wachstumspfad stellt jedoch eher den langfristigen Trend als eine Voraussage für einzelne Jahre dar. Für die Zeit von 1948 bis 1969 betrug die Wachstumsrate des realen Bruttosozialprodukts durchschnittlich 3,9 %. Von 1969 bis 1990 soll diese Größe auf 4,2 % ansteigen, weitgehend als Ergebnis einer beschleunigten Beschäftigungszunahme, die man für die nächsten 20 Jahre eher erwartet als man sie in den vergangenen 20 Jahren erwartet hätte.

Der ausschlaggebende Faktor für das Wachstum in den nächsten 20 Jahren wird im Ansteigen des BSP pro Kopf der Beschäftigtenzahl liegen, das auf Preisbasis 1971 von 12 500 Dollar 1970 auf 22 500 Dollar im Jahre 1990 steigen soll. Dies war auch für die Verdoppelung des BSP in den vorausgegangenen zwei Jahrzehnten ausschlaggebend. Eine der Voraussetzungen bei der Bestimmung des BSP ist eine sich nicht verändernde Produktivität im Bereich der öffentlichen

Hand mit Ausnahme der öffentlichen Unternehmungen. Die erzielte und die vorausberechnete Wachstumsrate des BSP bezogen auf die Anzahl der Beschäftigten stammt deshalb ganz aus dem privaten Bereich.

Die Zusammensetzung des BSP wird sich — für den Zeitraum der nächsten 20 Jahre betrachtet — nicht wesentlich verändern. Zyklusschwankungen bedingen große, kurzfristige Veränderungen, die sich vorrangig bei Investitionen und den Ausgaben für dauerhafte Konsumgüter bemerkbar machen. Wesentliche Schwankungen resultieren auch aus staatlichen Aktivitäten, besonders in Kriegszeiten.

Langfristig wird davon ausgegangen, daß die Konsumausgaben im Jahre 1990 ungefähr 60 % des BSP ausmachen; dies ist ungefähr der gleiche Anteil wie in den vergangenen 20 Jahren, abgesehen von den bereits erwähnten unregelmäßigen Schwankungen. Bis 1990 sollten deshalb die Konsumausgaben auf Preisbasis 1971 1,5 Billionen Dollar überschritten haben, was gegenüber heute einer Steigerungsrate von 135 % auf dem Waren- und Dienstleistungssektor entspricht. Es wird erwartet, daß der Anteil der öffentlichen Ausgaben bei 24 % des BSP konstant bleibt, das erbringt 1990 eine Gesamtsumme von 570 Mrd. Dollar.

Investitionen, die während der sechziger Jahre bei 15 % des BSP lagen, werden in den nächsten 20 Jahren schätzungsweise leicht abnehmen. Sie werden für 1990 mit 330 Mrd. Dollar veranschlagt. Ein relativ unbedeutender Anteil am BSP, der Außenhandelsüberschuß, wird in den ersten 10 Jahren vermutlich ansteigen und sich dann, absolut betrachtet, nach 1980 stabilisieren.

Workers in the boardrooms
Arbeiter im Vorstand

Wilson möchte den Einzelnen als freien Bürger an unternehmerischen und industriellen Entscheidungen, die ihn betreffen, beteiligen. Doch glauben viele Gewerkschaftler, daß Betriebsräte eine Farce, Mitbeteiligung der Arbeitnehmer ein Beschwichtigungsmittel und Mitbestimmung nichts weiter als Bauernfängerei sind. Wer hat recht? Wilson hat die Mitbestimmung der Arbeiter zu einem wichtigen Thema in seinen „Edinburgher" Reden gemacht. In Blackpool nannte er eine Reihe spezifischer Maßnahmen — unter anderem gemeinsame Entscheidungen über Planung und Produktionsmethoden im Betrieb; gesetzlich vorgeschriebene Betriebsräte; eine Dualstruktur im Top-Management mit Arbeitern in den Aufsichtsräten; bessere Betreuung durch die Gewerkschaften — ein bestechendes Aufgebot. Aber wird er damit einen Wandel in seinen eigenen Reihen erreichen — einmal ganz abgesehen von den erzkonservativen Vorstandsmitgliedern in den Betrieben?

Er hat wichtige Verbündete. Unter ihnen sind vielleicht überraschenderweise die Beamten in Brüssel. In der Mitbestimmungsfrage sind die meisten europäischen Länder Großbritannien weit voraus. Der EWG-Entwurf für ein neues Aktiengesetz sieht die von Wilson jetzt befürwortete Dualstruktur sowie eine gesetzliche Verankerung der Betriebsräte vor. Andere Länder, wie z. B. Westdeutschland und die Niederlande, haben jahrelange, wenn auch unterschiedliche Erfahrung mit diesem System. Ein Versuch lohnt sich auch hier, obwohl damit sicher nicht alle Streitpunkte und Enttäuschungen zu beseitigen sind.

Ohne es zu beabsichtigen, zeigte Wilson die Grenzen dessen auf, was die Mitbestimmung erreichen kann. In einer seiner Rundfunk- und Fernsehansprachen, in denen er zu Recht die Unmenschlichkeit der „Liquidationsgewinnler" anprangerte, erwähnte er voller Mitgefühl die Stahlarbeiter von Ebbw Vale, die er bei ihrer Demonstration in London gesehen hatte. Diese Stahlarbeiter gehören ausgerechnet dem britischen Industriezweig an, der über die am weitesten entwickelte Form der Mitbestimmung verfügt — eingeführt von Herrn Wilson selbst. Nach dem Gesetz von 1967 ernennt die British Steel Corporation Arbeitnehmervertreter für die Werksleitung. Das Experiment wird im großen und ganzen als Erfolg angesehen. Aber keine Form der Mitbestimmung — sei sie noch so weitgehend — kann eine Fabrik, ob Stahlwerk oder Schiffswerft, retten, wenn diese veraltet ist. Die Stahlindustrie hat in den letzten Jahren große technische Veränderungen erlebt. Vom technischen Standpunkt aus betrachtet, ist die Entscheidung, ein integriertes Werk mit einer Kapazität von 12 Mio. Tonnen am Ufer des Tees als nächste Stufe nach Scunthorpe zu errichten, durchaus richtig. Eine unabwendbare Folge dessen ist der drohende Niedergang von Ebbw Vale und Shotton. Wenn der britische Stahl konkurrenzfähig bleiben soll, muß die Stahlindustrie modernisieren. Wie beim Stahl ist auch die Lage in anderen Industriezweigen: Keine Mitbestimmung — und sei sie noch so umfassend — kann die Notwendigkeit solcher Entscheidungen abwenden, wenn nicht die gesamte britische Industrie hoffnungslos zurückbleiben soll.

Aber auch auf Seiten der Konservativen fängt man an zu denken. Eine brauchbare Studie — Bryan Cassidys „Workers on the Board" (Arbeiter im Vorstand) — wurde zum Preis von 15 p vom Conservative Political Centre herausgegeben. Hierin wird die Dualstruktur mit Interesse zur Kenntnis genommen. Zu ihrer Empfehlung aber konnte man sich nicht durchringen. Man erwartet einfach, daß mehr Betriebe dem Experiment der British Steel Corporation folgen. Gesetzlich vorgeschriebene Betriebsräte werden befürwortet, und mit Recht wird kritisiert, daß auf Vorstandsetagen und im Management zu viel Geheimhaltung betrieben wird.

Zwei herausragende Schwierigkeiten behindern den Fortschritt. Der Vorstand muß die vorgesehene Planung und zukünftige Verträge vertraulich und sachlich diskutieren können. Werden die Arbeiter ihren Vertretern diese Möglichkeit einräumen und davon Abstand nehmen, über jede Stufe der Verhandlungen Informationen zu verlangen? Außerdem muß schließlich der Gewinn auf Arbeiter, Aktionäre und Rücklagen aufgeteilt werden. Wird das ohne blutige Kämpfe möglich sein? Wilson, die Konservativen und viele andere tun klug daran, nach neuen Wegen zu suchen.

See How They Grow
Wie sie wachsen

Die alljährlich in FORTUNE erscheinende und in dieser Woche veröffentlichte Aufstellung über die 500 größten amerikanischen Industrieunternehmen ist eine Art Röntgenbild des Industriesektors der amerikanischen Wirtschaft: es beleuchtet Trends, die sich in den einzelnen Geschäftsberichten nur vage abzeichnen.

Unter den im vergangenen Jahr herausragenden Tendenzen ist zu erwähnen, daß die großen Unternehmen in doch verblüffender Weise fähig waren, bei steigendem Umsatz die Beschäftigtenzahl zu reduzieren, in ihrer Fusionsbereitschaft wiederum deutlich nachgelassen haben, und scheinbar beginnen, sich von Diversifikationsbemühungen abzuwenden.

Alles in allem war das Jahr 1971 für die 500 Unternehmen leidlich gut. Sie konnten ihre Gesamtumsätze um 8,4 % auf fast 503 Mrd. Dollar und die Gewinne um 8 % auf 23,4 Mrd. Dollar steigern. Diese Zahlen geben jedoch aufgrund der herausragenden Leistung von General Motors, die von einem Rekordjahr in der Autoindustrie profitieren, ein falsches Bild. Auf General Motors allein entfielen Dreiviertel des gesamten Gewinnzuwachses dieser Firmen. Andere Industrieriesen sind ebenfalls größer geworden. Sieben Unternehmen rückten in den einst exklusiven „Milliarden-Dollar-Umsatz-Klub" auf; dadurch stieg die Mitgliederzahl auf 127. Die neuen Mitglieder sind: Philip Morris, Nabisco, Bristol-Myers, Combustion Engineering, Campbell Soup, Iowa Beef Processors and CBS. Inzwischen konnte Standard Oil of California als 12. amerikanisches Unternehmen Umsätze von mehr als 5 Mrd. Dollar jährlich verzeichnen. Die 500 verstärkten auch leicht ihre Machtposition in der amerikanischen Wirtschaft — obwohl damit gleichzeitig Fragen hinsichtlich ihrer Leistungsfähigkeit aufgeworfen wurden. Im vergangenen Jahr verzeichneten sie 66 % des von Industrieunternehmen erzielten Gesamtumsatzes, verglichen mit 65 % im Jahr 1970 und etwas über 50 % vor 10 Jahren. Ihr Anteil an den Gewinnen aller Industrieunternehmen blieb jedoch bei 75 % nahezu unverändert konstant gegenüber 1970.

Offensichtlich haben kleinere Unternehmen ihre Rentabilität schneller als Großunternehmen gesteigert, wobei sich die Vermutung aufdrängt, daß einige der 500 — General Motors ausgenommen — ihre optimale Unternehmensgröße bereits überschritten haben.

In einer Beziehung haben die 500 ihre Leistungsfähigkeit deutlich bewiesen: sie reduzierten die Anzahl der Beschäftigten um 2 % (auf 14,3 Mio.) bei gleichzeitig wachsenden Umsatzzahlen. Als Ergebnis dessen stieg der durchschnittliche Umsatz pro Beschäftigten um 10 % auf 35,166 Dollar. General Motors, Ford und ITT, die drei größten Arbeitgeber, erhöhten alle die absolute Lohn- und Gehaltssumme. Aber General Electric, der viertgrößte, reduzierte die Anzahl seiner Arbeitnehmer um 8,5 %; 33 600 Beschäftigte konnten gehen.

Weiterhin ist bemerkenswert:

▶ Innerhalb der 500 fusionierten im vergangenen Jahr nur zwei: National Steel übernahm Granite City Steel und General Host übernahm Cudahy. Seit 1958 war das die niedrigste Zahl an Fusionen; vergleichsweise wurde 1968 eine Rekordzahl von 23 erreicht. Offenbar ist die vom Justizministerium gegen große Fusionen gerichtete Opposition dazu angetan, die Anzahl der Fusionen niedrig zu halten.

▶ 24 Gesellschaften schrieben im vergangenen Jahr einen erstaunlich hohen Verlust von 1,5 Mrd. Dollar ab, und einige der größten Abschreibungen betrafen die Kosten für die Entdiversifizierung aus nicht gewinnbringenden Bereichen. RCA schrieb 490 Mio. Dollar ab als erwarteten Verlust aus der Liquidation ihres Computergeschäfts. American Standard hat seine Abteilungen für Bergbauausrüstungen und Klimaanlagen aufgelöst und zieht sich aus dem Bereich der Erschließung von Erholungsgebieten und der Errichtung von Wohnmobilzentren sowie dem Wohnungsbau im Ausland zurück. Abschreibung: 122 Mio. Dollar.

The example of Shell International

Das Beispiel der Shell International

Die Besorgnis über das Wachstum multinationaler Gesellschaften und ihre mögliche Bedrohung für die Autorität der Regierung des Gastlandes hat in den letzten Jahren von den Entwicklungsländern auf die Industrieländer übergegriffen. Die Debatte konzentriert sich überwiegend auf die Macht, über die diese Unternehmen verfügen, und auf die für Regierungen bestehende Notwendigkeit, Mittel und Wege zu finden, mit denen diese Unternehmen zur Rechenschaft gezogen werden können.

Es kommt nicht oft vor, daß die Gesellschaften selbst einen Beitrag zu dieser Debatte leisten. Auch hört man nicht viel über die Beziehungen zwischen gastgebender Regierung und ausländischen Unternehmen, wenn die lokalen Aktivitäten einer multinationalen Gesellschaft in ernste Schwierigkeiten geraten und in ihrem Umfang eingeschränkt werden müssen. Dies ist vielleicht noch nicht sehr oft geschehen, aber die in einem konkreten Fall aufgetretenen praktischen Probleme werden von einem der Direktoren von Shell International, Geoffrey Chandler, in der neuesten Ausgabe der Zeitschrift „Moorgate and Wallstreet" beschrieben. Obwohl sich dieser Fall in Trinidad ereignete, während Chandler dort als Hauptgeschäftsführer der Shell tätig war, sind die Lehren auch auf Situationen anwendbar, die in nicht so weiter Ferne auftreten.

Trinidad war einer der ersten Ölproduzenten der Welt. Aber reiche Ölvorkommen andernorts und der Trend, Raffinerien auf den Hauptabsatzmärkten zu errichten, hatten die Ölfelder und Raffinerien der Insel Anfang der 60er Jahre weitgehend konkurrenzunfähig gemacht. Um eine Betriebsverkleinerung zu vermeiden, versuchte die Shell, neue Verfahren für die Gewinnung von Rohöl aus den minderwertigen Vorkommen der Insel zu entwickeln. Die neuen Methoden erwiesen sich als technisch durchführbar, boten jedoch keinerlei Aussicht auf Rentabilität. Deshalb bestand die einzige Alternative darin, die Zahl der Arbeitskräfte um die Hälfte zu reduzieren — eine Aussicht, die bei einer Arbeitslosigkeit von 15 % auf der Insel und von 30 % unter den Schulabgängern weder die gastgebende Regierung, noch die mächtige lokale Gewerkschaft ohne weiteres akzeptieren würden.

Geleitet von den Empfehlungen der ILO wandte das Unternehmen die — man sollte fast sagen klassische — Verhaltensweise der Arbeitgeber im Falle von überschüssigen Arbeitskräften an. Einige der von Geoffrey Chandler beschriebenen Maßnahmen sind nur in einem Entwicklungsland angebracht — so etwa die Rückführung ausländischer Staatsbürger, Reisezuschüsse für solche Arbeitnehmer, die auf andere karibische Inseln zurückzukehren wünschten sowie der Verkauf von Ausrüstungen für Nebenarbeiten wie Drucken, Reinigung und Gebäudeinstandhaltung zu niedrigen Preisen an solche Arbeitnehmer, die sich selbständig machen wollten.

Ob eine Gesellschaft Umschulungsmöglichkeiten bieten oder fördern und ihren Arbeitnehmern behilflich sein sollte, neue Arbeitsplätze zu finden, hängt offensichtlich von den örtlichen Gegebenheiten ab. Aber mehrere andere von Geoffrey Chandler beschriebene Maßnahmen könnten für jedes Einschränkungsprogramm von Vorteil sein. Neben einer deutlichen und vollständigen Information auf allen Ebenen ist es auch wichtig, dafür zu sorgen, daß Manager und leitende Angestellte von der Notwendigkeit und Fairneß der geplanten Maßnahmen überzeugt sind, weil man sonst möglicherweise nicht auf ihre Mitarbeit zählen kann. Gleichzeitig sollten Einsparungen an der Spitze ebenso vorgenommen werden wie am unteren Ende der Leiter. Und da die Bereitstellung von einmaligen Abfindungen zusätzlich zu den auf übliche Weise akkumulierten Beträgen als Anreiz für eine freiwillige Pensionierung zu einer unausgewogenen Alterspyramide führen kann, dürfte es überdies wünschenswert sein, das Pensionsmindestalter zu senken, ohne gleichzeitig die Bezüge zu mindern.

Da das Unternehmen in dieser besonderen Situation Fairneß und ein Gespür für die menschlichen Belange bewies, gewann es die Zustimmung seiner Arbeitnehmer, der Gewerkschaft und der gastgebenden Regierung und erreichte somit sein Hauptziel. Die Schwierigkeiten, mit denen ein multinationales Unternehmen konfrontiert wird, unterscheiden sich nur größenmäßig von denen eines nationalen Unternehmens. Aber vielleicht besteht die Lehre dieses und anderer Beispiele massiver Betriebseinschränkungen — wie Chandler selbst feststellt — darin, daß Unternehmen auf wirtschaftliche, technologische oder wettbewerbsmäßige Veränderungen sofort reagieren und nicht so lange warten sollten, bis „Amputationen" größeren Ausmaßes unvermeidlich werden.

On with Exxon

Neu auf dem Markt: Exxon

Neben Coke, Jeep, Mace, Band-Aid und Levi gehört ESSO zu den berühmtesten Markennamen der Welt. Von der Standard Oil Company (New Jersey) wird dieser Name im Ausland und in vielen Teilen der Vereinigten Staaten verwendet, in denen Humble Oil and Refining Company, die heimische Produktions- und Vertriebsgesellschaft, ESSO als Markenname benutzt. Die Schwierigkeit liegt darin, daß seit 1911, als der ehemalige Standard Oil Konzern aufgelöst wurde, gesetzliche Restriktionen es Humble unmöglich machen, den Namen ESSO in 20 Staaten einzuführen. In manchen Teilen der Südstaaten und des Westens verwendet die Gesellschaft die Handelsbezeichnung Enco oder — wie in Ohio — Humble.

Nachdem man sich jahrzehntelang in den USA mit Werbe- und Marketingproblemen, die durch eine Vielzahl von Warenzeichen hervorgerufen werden, herumgeschlagen hat, erklärte jetzt ein Vertreter der Firma Humble, man habe sich endgültig auf einen Kompromiß geeinigt. Vom kommenden Januar an wird das Unternehmen unter Exxon Company firmieren, und im Juli werden seine drei Benzinsorten in Exxon, Exxon plus und Exxon extra umbenannt. Mit einem Kostenaufwand von 25 Mio. Dollar wird in einer Werbekampagne die Namensänderung in der Öffentlichkeit bekanntgemacht. Weitere 10 Mio. Dollar werden aufgewendet, um an den mehr als 25 000 Tankstellen der Firma die Namensschilder zu ändern und auf Briefköpfen, an Zapfsäulen und Lastwagen die Bezeichnung Exxon anzubringen.

Der Name ist das Ergebnis mehr als fünfjähriger linguistischer Analysen, psychologischer Tests über Verbraucherverhalten und Marktforschung. In der Forschungsabteilung der Firma Humble wurden Tausende mit Hilfe von Computern ausgewählte Buchstaben-Kombinationen und Wörter in 55 Sprachen untersucht, bis eine Kombination gefunden wurde, die anscheinend im Gedächtnis der Verbraucher haften bleibt und in keiner anderen Sprache eine obszöne oder irreführende Bedeutung hat. Ein wichtiger Schritt war die Erkenntnis, daß es außer dem Maltesischen keine Sprache gibt, die in einem Wort eine Kombination von zwei aufeinanderfolgenden X kennt. Da später der neue Markenname von dem Unternehmen vielleicht auch im Ausland verwendet wird, wurde Enco, eine der derzeit gebräuchlichen Handelsbezeichnungen, bereits im Frühstadium abgelehnt. Im Japanischen bedeutet es nämlich „Wagen mit abgewürgtem Motor".

Facing the economic facts of life
Die wirtschaftlichen Gegebenheiten des Lebens vor Augen

Die jährliche Währungskrise flaut ab inmitten der üblichen gegenseitigen Beschuldigungen, der üblichen Rufe nach neuen Bestimmungen zur Verhinderung von Spekulationen und der üblichen Kritik an Gold- und Devisenreserven und an der verhältnismäßig uneinsichtigen Haltung der Länder, die zu viele Waren oder zu viel Geld exportieren. Weil diese Kritik so alltäglich geworden ist, ist man versucht, sie mit einer Geste unaussprechlicher Langeweile abzutun und anzunehmen, daß alles mehr oder weniger so weitertrottet wie bisher.

Nach so vielen unverständlichen Warnungen sind kaum noch die direkt Betroffenen davon zu überzeugen, daß es dieses Mal anders ist; dieses Mal ist die Situation wirklich gefährlich.

In der protektionistischen Haltung des amerikanischen Kongresses und in seiner Feindseligkeit gegenüber Präsident Nixon liegt die akuteste und offenkundige Gefahr. Präsident Nixon kann nur dann über Außenhandelsprobleme verhandeln, wenn er vom Kongreß mit Vollmachten ausgestattet wird; der Kongreß scheint nur gewillt, ihn mit einem zweischneidigen Schwert auszurüsten, welches benutzt werden kann, um sowohl den Handel als auch die Handelsschranken abzubauen — und der Präsident ist mehr als gewillt, sowohl Drohungen als auch Friedensangebote anzuwenden, um seine Handelspartner zu ernsthaften Verhandlungen zu bewegen. Eine Gefahr besteht auch in der Vietnamisierung der Außenhandelsprobleme.

Auf diese Drohung mit heftigem Antiamerikanismus zu reagieren ist leicht, und diese Reaktion war letzte Woche in Brüssel bereits zu spüren. Die amerikanische Ungeduld ist jedoch keineswegs unvernünftig. Auf dieser Seite des Atlantik will man anscheinend nicht einsehen, daß wir vor Problemen stehen, die sich nicht durch einige wenige währungspolitische Instrumente und das Feilschen um Handelsregelungen lösen lassen. Neue Regelungen werden nicht die Logik beseitigen können, die vorschreibt, daß die Mobilität des Geldes nach wie vor erhalten bleiben muß, schon einfach deshalb, weil

Handel und Industrie international sind; daß — solange die Inflation ein ungelöstes Problem darstellt — Unsicherheit über die Bewertung des Geldes herrscht und daß ein starkes und andauerndes Ungleichgewicht Strukturfehler im Außenhandel widerspiegelt, die offensichtlich nicht durch den Federstrich eines Bankiers zu beseitigen sind.

Wir haben nur eine Wahl: zu lernen, mit diesen Problemen zu leben bis grundlegende Lösungen gefunden sind, oder sie durch Zuflucht zu verstärkter handels- und währungspolitischer Isolation zu beseitigen.

Jedes Land ist anscheinend durchaus in der Lage, das Problem von seiner eigenen Warte aus zu sehen: Großbritannien argumentiert zu Recht, daß das Pfund nicht erneut gestützt werden kann, ehe nicht die Kosten im Inland stabilisiert sind; Japan weist mit gleichem Recht darauf hin, daß sein unausgeglichener Handel eine unausgeglichene Wirtschaft widerspiegelt, welche von industrieller Expansion auf soziale Expansion umdirigiert werden muß. Aber wir werden ungeduldig, wenn es sich um die Probleme anderer handelt — die Franzosen beim britischen Floating, die ganze Welt bei der „Bedrohung" durch die hervorragenden Konsumgüter aus Japan.

Sollen diese Probleme gelöst werden, so müssen sie erkannt werden. Wir brauchen ein Währungssystem, welches durch nicht zu vermeidende Unsicherheitsfaktoren nicht umgeworfen wird; Einvernehmen darüber, wie andauerndes Ungleichgewicht zunächst finanziert und auf längere Sicht korrigiert werden soll; Einvernehmen darüber (so die Argumente der Amerikaner), welche vorübergehenden Maßnahmen zum Schutz eines sich neu entwickelnden oder eines notleidenden Industriezweiges legitim sind; und Einvernehmen darüber, welchen Bestimmungen die Tätigkeit multinationaler Firmen unterliegen soll.

Wir scheinen jedoch nichts anderes zu bekommen, als uralte Heilmittel für Währungsprobleme, Angriffsmanöver auf den Handel und die Weigerung, die langfristigen Struktur- und Energieversorgungsprobleme sowie die Probleme der Verteidigungslasten, die durch die Krisen aufgeworfen werden, überhaupt zu sehen. Großbritannien mit seiner weltoffenen Wirtschaft sollte als erstes Land strategisch vorgehen und seinen Partnern erklären, daß wirtschaftliches Fehlverhalten nicht von jemandem beseitigt werden kann, der sich wie ein unartiges Kind benimmt.

How to Fight Inflation
Wie man die Inflation bekämpft

Das Inflationsproblem, von dem kein Industrieland gegenwärtig frei ist, ist ein politisches Problem. Der Grund für die weltweite Inflation ist nicht darin zu suchen, daß die Wirtschaftswissenschaft keine Möglichkeit bietet, den Wert einer Währung zu erhalten, sondern daß die politischen Maßnahmen, die zur Aufrechterhaltung einer Währung erforderlich sind, für demokratische Wähler nicht annehmbar sind und selbst in autoritären Systemen zu unerträglichem Druck führen würden.

Die große Wirkung der Inflation liegt darin, daß sie zu einer Umschichtung der Kaufkraft führt. Man spricht sehr offen über die Kosten der Inflation und darüber, daß man mehr für Fleisch oder Brot oder Häuser bezahlen muß. Man spricht nicht so offen darüber, wie man persönlich von der Inflation profitiert, obwohl die Inflation nicht anhalten würde, wenn nicht sehr mächtige Gruppen unserer Gesellschaft davon profitierten. Wenn jeder, wie er vorgibt, wirklich gegen die Inflation wäre, dann würde der politische Druck, der sich gegen stabile Währungen richtet, nicht existieren und es wäre relativ einfach, die Preisstabilität in der westlichen Welt sicherzustellen.

Da die Inflation ein politisches Problem ist, kann sie nur mit politischen Mitteln gelöst werden. Sie stellt jede Regierung vor die denkbar größten Probleme. Die Wähler sind weitgehend entrüstet über steigende Preise, sie empören sich auch über Maßnahmen zur Deflation und in der Einkommenspolitik, die die steigenden Preise eindämmen sollen. In einem Land, das wie Deutschland in den zwanziger Jahren, eine galoppierende Inflation erlebt hat, mag die Öffentlichkeit eine Inflation so stark fürchten, daß die Regierung es sich erlauben kann, konsequent im Interesse der Preisstabilität zu handeln. Dies könnte auch in England der Fall sein, aber so weit ist es noch nicht.

Hat jedoch die Inflation erst einmal den jetzigen Stand erreicht, steht eine Regierung vor einer äußerst unangenehmen Wahl. Duldet sie weiterhin den Preisanstieg, kann sie damit rechnen, die nächste Wahl wegen des Preisproblems zu verlieren. Wenn sie eine Politik betreibt, die ausreicht, die Preissteigerungsrate zu reduzieren, von dem Ziel der Geldwertstabilität ganz zu schweigen, kann sie damit rechnen, die nächste Wahl aufgrund des Arbeitslosenproblems zu verlieren. Die Labourregierung war unfähig, dieses Problem zu lösen und schaufelte sich damit tatsächlich ihr eigenes Grab. Die derzeitige Regierung befindet sich angesichts einer immer drückenderen Inflation und einer höheren Arbeitslosenquote sogar in noch größeren Schwierigkeiten.

Zweifelsohne hat der Premierminister Recht mit seiner Behauptung, daß es kein Allheilmittel gibt, das sich Einkommenspolitik nennt und welches das Dilemma für ihn lösen wird. Auf jeden Fall hängt die Fähigkeit der Regierung, eine Einkommenspolitik zu betreiben, von ihrem politischen Verhältnis zu den Gewerkschaften und der Masse der Gewerkschaftler ab. Das soll jedoch nicht heißen, daß die gesetzlichen Lohn- und Preiskontrollen als Teil einer Politik zur Inflationsbekämpfung nichts zu leisten vermögen.

Wirklich sonderbar ist die Tatsache, daß die Regierung weder eine Einkommenspolitik, noch eine Währungspolitik betrieben hat, obwohl diese die klassischen Mittel zur Inflationsbekämpfung darstellen. Es ist wesentlich, daß eine Regierung ein umfassendes Anti-Inflations-Programm verabschiedet; unserer Meinung nach sollte dieses Programm den Einsatz verschiedenartiger Mittel beinhalten, weil eine einzelne politische Maßnahme allein nicht entscheidend wirken kann.

Die unkontrollierte Währungspolitik der vergangenen zwölf Monate ist über das hinaus gegangen, was für die Steigerung der Nachfrage und Reduzierung der Arbeitslosigkeit nötig war, und konnte jedenfalls das Vertrauen in die Wirtschaft bis jetzt nicht wieder herstellen. Die Währungspolitik war 1969 und Anfang 1970 mit Bestimmtheit fast zu strikt, im vergangenen Jahr mit noch größerer Bestimmtheit zu lasch.

Die Regierung hätte versuchen sollen, soviel Einfluß wie möglich auf den Bereich der Einkommenspolitik zu nehmen.

Eine gesetzlich fixierte Einkommenspolitik mit der Möglichkeit, unvernünftige Regelungen auszusetzen und vorübergehende Einfrierungen und Abkühlungsperioden zu verordnen, wenn die Inflation besonders stark wird, sollte normaler Bestandteil einer nationalen Währungspolitik sein. Die Anwendung einer vernünftigen, in Schranken gehaltenen Währungspolitik in freiwilligem Zusammenwirken mit industriellen Interessenverbänden, wie es die Regierung mit dem CBI zustande gebracht hat, und die Realisierung einer Einkommenspolitik, die zwar limitiert aber eindeutig gesetzlich fixiert ist, bietet die beste Aussicht auf Milderung des inflationären Übels. Diese Maßnahmen müssen ergänzt werden durch eine Politik sozialer Gerechtigkeit und, wenn möglich, durch wirtschaftliches Wachstum, welches das von der Inflation zerstörte Gefühl nationaler Gerechtigkeit wieder herstellt.

Das politische Grundproblem bliebe dennoch bestehen. Die gesellschaftlichen Kräfte, die dazu neigen, die Inflation zu schüren, sind sehr stark. In den meisten Ländern sind sie derzeit wohl stärker als eine demokratische Regierung, der eine starke Opposition gegenübersteht, und die die Wahlen gewinnen muß. In einigen Ländern sind sie stärker als autoritäre Regime, die mit politischem Druck und Spannungen ebenso fertig werden müssen wie demokratische Regierungen. Bestenfalls kann man unter diesen Umständen auf einen klugen, beweglichen und mit List geführten Rückzug hoffen mit dem Ziel, den Schaden und die Inflationsrate zu mindern, und ohne große Illusionen von möglichen Siegen.

Bonn hopes to deflate the boom

Bonn hofft, die Hochkonjunktur in den Griff zu bekommen

In dieser Woche kündigte die westdeutsche Regierung eine Reihe von Steuererhöhungen als Teil eines Programms an, mit dessen Hilfe die Kaufkraft um etwa 840 Mio. Pfund reduziert werden soll.

Von Juli an wird die Benzinsteuer um 5 Pfennig pro Liter (ungefähr 3 p pro Gallone) erhöht. Damit wird Westdeutschland den zweiten Platz in der europäischen Benzinpreisliste einnehmen. Ein Liter Normalbenzin wird DM 0,72 kosten (in Italien vergleichsweise DM 0,85) und liegt damit leicht über den Preisen in Frankreich.

Die Einkommensteuer wird für Bezieher höherer Einkommen ebenfalls erhöht. Ein Jahr lang, beginnend mit dem 1. Juli, werden Ledige mit einem zu versteuernden Einkommen von mehr als DM 100 000 und Verheiratete, deren zu versteuerndes Einkommen mindestens zweimal so hoch ist, eine zusätzliche Steuer von 10 % zahlen müssen. Diese Einnahmen werden zunächst stillgelegt und später für ein neues Modell benutzt, das Vermögensbildung ermöglichen soll.

Die Regierung legt auch eine Stabilitätsanleihe im Gesamtwert von ca. 560 Mio. Pfund auf, die bei der Bundesbank hinterlegt werden. Man will so den Geldumlauf reduzieren und die Inflation eindämmen.

Auf einer Kabinettssitzung am Samstag wurde ein Budget in Höhe von DM 120 Mrd. für das Jahr 1973 gebilligt. Dies stellt eine Erhöhung von 9,7 % dar mit entsprechender Auswirkung auf die Inflationsrate.

A Secret IMF Proposal for Monetary Reform Urges Radical Changes
In einem Geheimvorschlag des IWF zur Währungsreform werden radikale Veränderungen gefordert

Nach Finanzminister Conally gibt es keinen geheimen Grund dafür, daß ernsthafte Gespräche über eine Weltwährungsreform bisher nicht stattgefunden haben. Es ist einfach die mangelnde Vorstellung davon, was andere Nationen wollen.

Jetzt hat man jedoch mehr noch als nur eine Vorstellung — einen recht detaillierten Vorschlag sogar, in Form eines sorgsam gehüteten internationalen Memorandums der 120 Mitglieder des Internationalen Währungsfonds.

Der von einem Mitarbeiterstab des IWF entworfene Vorschlag findet zunehmend günstige Aufnahme und wird unter den hiesigen Botschaften und den wichtigsten Finanzministerien der ganzen Welt vertraulich herumgereicht. Wie die Autoren jedoch selbst zugeben, wird er von einigen Ländern als radikal und unannehmbar kritisiert werden.

Wahrscheinlich werden die Vereinigten Staaten diese Ansicht am ehesten vertreten, weil das Dokument des IWF so durchgreifende Forderungen für die USA beinhaltet wie:

— sie können nicht wie bisher Dollarberge im Ausland entstehen lassen und müssen die künftig ins Ausland abfließenden Dollar zu festgesetzten Terminen mit Gold oder anderen Reserven zurückkaufen

— sie sollten, wie jeder andere Staat auch, bereit sein, die Dollarparität einer veränderten Lage sofort anzupassen

— sie sollten sich darauf einstellen, daß die derzeit in Milliardenbeträgen bei anderen Regierungen liegenden Dollar an den IWF abgegeben werden und nach und nach von Amerika zurückgekauft werden müssen

— sie müssen sich von dem Gedanken frei machen, daß andere Länder dazu da sind, ihre Zahlungsbilanzüberschüsse zusammenzustreichen und daß die Rolle des Goldes als internationale Reserve bald beendet sein wird.

Gerade gegen die Lücken im Vorschlag des IWF wird die Regierung Nixon die meisten Einwände erheben. Nicht erwähnt sind „Sanktionen", mit denen andere Länder gezwungen werden können, ihre Zahlungsbilanzüberschüsse schnell zu bereinigen, so daß die USA sich nicht zu sehr um einen Ausgleich ihrer Defizite bemühen müssen.

Mehrere Aspekte des IWF-Vorschlags werden jedoch sogar in den Vereinigten Staaten von verschiedenen Kreisen begrüßt. Regierungskreise, die sich aus Angst vor Devisenspekulationen ruhig verhalten, sind generell der Meinung, daß in Zukunft Dollarabwertungen routinemäßig zur Verbesserung der Handelsbilanzen eingesetzt werden sollten. Henry Reuss, demokratischer Vertreter im Repräsentantenhaus und Leiter der Internationalen Arbeitsgruppe des Gemeinsamen Wirtschaftsausschusses ist der Meinung, daß das Dokument des IWF „als Grundlage für Reformverhandlungen" dienen könnte, auch wenn die USA nicht „mit jedem Punkt einverstanden" sind. Von Experten wird hinzugefügt, daß dieses oder nahezu jedes andere, bisher bekannte Instrument wirksam eingesetzt werden könnte, wenn andere Länder in den Bereichen Handel, Steuer usw. die notwendigen Schritte unternähmen, um den USA aus ihren ständigen Zahlungsbilanzdefiziten herauszuhelfen.

Unumstritten ist das Hauptziel des IWF-Plans. Er soll das im Dezember 1971 in aller Eile auf der Washingtoner Währungskonferenz ausgearbeitete Währungssystem durch ein „für die nächsten 15 bis 20 Jahre" gültiges Konzept ersetzen...

Umstritten ist jedoch, zumindest bei der Regierung Nixon, die im IWF-Bericht beschworene Dringlichkeit. Die auf der Washingtoner Währungskonferenz entstandenen Neuregelungen, nach denen andere Länder nach wie vor Dollar ankaufen ohne die Sicherheit, diese in Gold oder andere Reserven umzutauschen, „spiegeln nicht die wirtschaftlichen und politischen Gegebenheiten wider", heißt es in dem Bericht. Er warnt davor, daß ein weiteres Festhalten an den derzeitigen Bestimmungen, die Gefahr einer nicht beabsichtigten „Aufspaltung der Welt in eine Reihe von Währungsblöcken mit... den damit verbundenen wirtschaftlichen und politischen Risiken" ... in sich birgt.

Wie ein Diplomat behauptet, sind die Vorstellungen des IWF den Ansichten der britischen Regierung „nicht unähnlich"; beide betonen die stark nachlassende Bedeutung des Dollars im offiziellen internationalen Handel. Die Regierungen würden anstelle des Dollar oder der Währung eines anderen Landes ein aufpoliertes Modell der vom IWF geschaffenen „Sonderziehungsrechte" als wichtigste Form internationaler Währungsreserven benutzen.

Der Vorschlag des IWF würde jedoch weiter gehen als jemals in offiziellen britischen Erklärungen zu lesen war. In der Absicht, den Dollar des letzten Restes seines privilegierten Status zu berauben, wird darin angeregt, die Rolle des Dollar als wichtigste „Interventionswährung" ebenfalls zu beenden.

Im Gegensatz dazu schlägt der IWF versuchsweise vor, in mehr als einer Währung „symmetrisch zu intervenieren" ...

Im Dokument heißt es, diese Veränderung würde für die übrigen Beteiligten „die Sonderstellung des Dollar ganz und gar beseitigen". Weil dies jedoch einen „abrupten Bruch mit der Praxis der Vergangenheit" bedeute, müßten erst andere Reformen durchgesetzt werden, heißt es in dem Bericht weiter.

Ein derartiger Schlag gegen den Dollar könnte in internationalen Währungskreisen weitgehende Unterstützung finden. Im Ausland wird das Verhalten der USA abgelehnt, weil das ungehinderte Ausfließen des Dollar die eigenen Inflationsprobleme verschlimmert ...

Der neue „Interventionsplan" soll aber mehr erreichen als nur Rachegelüste stillen. Die Überlegungen innerhalb des IWF laufen vielmehr darauf hinaus, daß ein deratiger Plan die Schwelle zu einer Ära bilden würde, in der andere Länder bei der Bildung von Währungsreserven nicht mehr auf zufällige Zahlungsbilanzdefizite der USA angewiesen wären. Experten behaupten, mit diesem Vorschlag würde ein geordnetes System entstehen und die Rolle des IWF als eine Art Weltbank durch zusätzliche Schaffung von SZR zum Zwecke der Reservebildung intensiviert.

Die Verantwortlichen innerhalb des IWF sind deshalb gegen eine neue Währung wie sie die Länder des Gemeinsamen Marktes letztlich schaffen könnten und die dann die Rolle einer Reservewährung einnehmen könnte. Warnend wird in dem Bericht „eine möglicherweise gefährliche Expansion" einiger „aufkommender" Reservewährungen bereits als Bedrohung angesehen. Wenn ein Land als Bank für andere Länder auftritt, so kann es nach der übereinstimmenden Meinung vieler Beobachter leicht zu einem panikartigen Zusammenbruch kommen, wenn zu viele Einlagen gleichzeitig abgezogen werden.

Ironischerweise, so der Bericht, ist das seit 15. August angewandte Währungssystem „mehr auf den Dollar ausgerichtet denn je". Obwohl die USA nicht mehr verpflichtet sind, Dollar in Gold auszugleichen, kaufen ausländische Regierungen noch immer Dollar an, um die Währungskurse relativ stabil zu halten. Die Dollarbestände dieser Regierungen beliefen sich Ende Januar 1972 auf 47,9 Mrd. Dollar, im Vergleich zu 33 Mrd. Dollar im vergangenen Juli und 20 Mrd. Dollar Ende Januar 1971.

Um diesen „Überhang" an Dollar im Ausland zu beseitigen, schlägt der Bericht vor, anderen Ländern „die Option (und vielleicht manchmal auch die Verpflichtung)" zu geben, durch sogenannte „Konsolidierungsabkommen" diese Guthaben in SZR umzuwandeln. Das bedeutet im Grunde genommen, daß der IWF die Dollar aufnehmen und dafür SZR in beträchtlicher Höhe ausgeben müßte.

Um diese Dollarbestände im Ausland nicht ins Unermeßliche wachsen zu lassen, wird im IWF-Bericht ein jährlicher oder sogar vierteljährlicher „Zwangsumtausch" vorgeschlagen. Das bedeutet, daß das amerikanische Schatzamt, sollte z. B. Deutschland in drei Monaten 500 Mio. US-Dollar ansammeln, diesen Betrag in Gold, SZR oder anderen Währungen bis zu einem festen Termin „ausspucken" müßte, um die Dollar zurückzukaufen. Um ihre Verpflichtung einzuhalten, könnten die USA bei anderen Ländern oder beim IWF Anleihen aufnehmen.

Der Bericht räumt ein, daß man von den USA keine Zustimmung zu einer derartigen „Guthabenfinanzierung" ihrer Zahlungsbilanzdefizite erwarten könne, „es sei denn, sie könnten mit einer Wechselkurspolitik als ein Heilmittel für ihre Defizite rechnen". Jetzt da der Kongreß dem Ersuchen Präsident Nixons um Abwertung des Dollars zugestimmt hat — der Preis pro Unze Feingold wurde von 35 auf 38 Dollar heraufgesetzt — sind, dem Bericht zufolge „Veränderungen der Dollarparität zu einem anerkannten Instrument der Wechselkursmanipulation geworden". Dem IWF bleibt als Aufgabe nur noch, die zukünftigen Bandbreiten für den Dollar und die anderen Währungen zu fixieren.

What Marshall Aid did for Europe

Was der Marshallplan für Europa getan hat

Es war ein schlechtes Jahr für die Marshallhilfe. In den 25 Jahren, die uns von der Rede des Außenministers der Vereinigten Staaten, George Marshall, in der Harvard Universität trennen, haben wir zunächst einen Prozeß ständiger Expansion der wirtschaftlichen und militärischen Macht Amerikas erlebt, der nun übergeht in einen scheinbar unvermeidlichen Prozeß sinkenden wirtschaftlichen Einflusses und moralischer Einbußen.

In Südostasien nähert sich das Syndrom der Marshallhilfe, wie es Professor Galbraith nennt — messianische Einflußnahme gestützt auf unbegrenzte Geldmittel — dramatisch einem Höhepunkt. In Westeuropa hat die Abwendung des internationalen Handels vom Dollar eine kritische Phase erreicht, eine Umkehr des internationalen Handels, die aus rein taktischen Gründen die Richtigkeit der Washingtoner Strategie des Kalten Krieges nach 1945 für die Vereinigten Staaten in Frage stellt.

Diejenigen in Washington, die die Marshallplanjahre miterlebt haben, müssen mit widersprüchlichen Gefühlen auf die Entwicklungen der vergangenen 25 Jahre zurückblicken. Das Ziel Marshalls und vieler seiner engsten Berater, durch Zerstörung der traditionellen europäischen Handelsstruktur die „kommunistischen" Staaten Europas zu isolieren, hat jedoch in Westeuropa eine wachsende Abneigung gegen die Macht des Dollars und auch einen Drang zur wirtschaftlichen Integration als Mittel zur Beseitigung dieser Macht gefördert.

Der Marshallplan trug zur Schwächung der osteuropäischen Wirtschaften bei; er brachte gleichzeitig Westeuropa auf einen Expansionskurs, der jetzt die wirtschaftliche Stellung der Vereinigten Staaten in ihren Grundfesten bedroht. Es gibt sicher kritische Betrachter in Washington, die jetzt sowohl die enorme Höhe der Marshallplanhilfe als auch die damit verbundene Spaltungsdoktrin in Frage stellen, denn die Geldmittel haben einen ernst zu nehmenden wirtschaftlichen

Rivalen erzeugt, während die kompromißlose antikommunistische Haltung schließlich zu einer Vereinigung von zehn[1]) der dynamischsten Staaten des Kontinents geführt hat.

1947 hatte Westeuropa ein sehr großes Leistungsbilanzdefizit und einen Fehlbetrag von 1,5 Mrd. Dollar bei den Kapitalbewegungen. Trotz der Hilfe der Vereinigten Staaten in Höhe von 6 Mrd. Dollar fielen die westeuropäischen Währungsreserven im Laufe des Jahres um 2,5 Mrd. Dollar. Auf der Pariser Konferenz wurde ein Zahlungsdefizit von 22 Mrd. Dollar für vier Jahre bis 1952 eingeplant. Das Europäische Wiederaufbauprogramm (ERP) sollte diese Zahlungslücke schließen; für das erste Jahr dieses Programms bewilligte der amerikanische Kongreß über 5 Mrd. Dollar.

Als Folge des Europäischen Wiederaufbauprogramms wurde der gesamteuropäische Handel nach und nach durch den Dollarhandel ersetzt, und die europäische Wirtschaft wurde in zwei Teile gespalten, eine Teilung, die durch die Entstehung der Europäischen Gemeinschaft festgeschrieben wurde. Das Hauptkriterium für die Zuteilung von ERP-Mitteln an das jeweilige Land war „die zu erwartende Höhe seines Defizits gegenüber dem Dollarraum".

Diese Formel beinhaltete somit einen Anreiz für den Handel mit dem Dollarblock, denn je größer das Defizit gegenüber dem Dollar, desto größer der Anspruch eines Landes auf ERP-Mittel-Zuteilung. Von 1947 bis 1950 finanzierten die Vereinigten Staaten 25 % der gesamten Importe Westeuropas, wobei nahezu 70 % dieser Importe aus dem Dollarblock kamen.

Von dem Leistungsbilanzdefizit im Jahre 1947 in Höhe von 7 Mrd. Dollar rührten über 5 Mrd. Dollar von Importen aus den USA her. Mit dem Marshallplan sollte dieses Dollardefizit durch Dollarhilfe vermindert werden. Da der Devisenmangel das kritische Problem darstellte, gingen westeuropäische Exporte zwangsläufig in Gebiete, wo reichlich Devisenreserven vorhanden waren, nämlich in die Vereinigten Staaten. Von 1947 bis 1957 stiegen folglich die westeuropäischen Exporte in den Dollarraum sprunghaft um 400 %.

[1]) Der Autor bezieht offensichtlich Norwegen mit ein. — Anm. d. Übers.

Das politische Grundprinzip der amerikanischen Hilfspolitik — gestützt auf die Weisungen des Kongresses, die Hilfe an ein Handelsembargo gegenüber Ländern unter kommunistischer Herrschaft zu knüpfen — war von noch größerer Tragweite, weil es jegliche Aussicht auf Verbesserung des Handels mit Osteuropa im Keim erstickte und den Grundstein für die wirtschaftliche Spaltung des europäischen Kontinents legte.

Mitte der 50er Jahre schien der Kalte Krieg im Wirtschaftsbereich gewonnen. Osteuropa war isoliert, Westeuropa in wirtschaftlicher Hinsicht beinahe eine Zweigstelle der Vereinigten Staaten. Der britische Handel war stark auf Dollarexporte gerichtet, Westeuropa nach Amerika orientiert.

Im Zuge dieses Prozesses nahmen die Direktinvestitionen auf Dollarbasis in Westeuropa zwangsläufig explosionsartige Form an: 1950 betrugen sie 118 Mrd. Dollar, 1963 hatten sie 406 Mrd. Dollar erreicht, eine Steigerung von 244 % in 13 Jahren. Amerikas Kampfansage an den Kommunismus war zu einer Herausforderung für Westeuropa geworden.

Seit 1958, dem Gründungsjahr der EWG, wurde diese Entwicklung immer deutlicher. 1958 lag der Außenhandel der EWG-Länder untereinander bei nur 30 %; 1971 betrug der Außenhandel zwischen den EWG-Ländern zum ersten Mal mehr als 50 % des Gesamtaußenhandels der EWG. Der Beitritt Großbritanniens wird entscheidend zu dieser Entwicklung beitragen: seit 1958 ist der britische Handel mit Westeuropa um 300 % gestiegen, ein Aufschwung, der sich mit der allmählichen Beseitigung der Handelsschranken weiter beschleunigen wird.

Demgegenüber ging 1971 der Export der Vereinigten Staaten in die EWG-Länder trotz einer 11 %igen Erhöhung der EWG-Importe insgesamt real zurück. Da die erweiterte EWG in bezug auf Nahrungsmittel und Technologie an Autarkie gewinnt, werden sich die Importe aus den Vereinigten Staaten weiter verringern. All das bestätigt immer mehr, wie recht Richard Cooper, Professor an der Yale Universität hatte, als er vor dem Plenum des Kongresses sagte: „Da die Europäische Gemeinschaft bei weitem den größten Handel mit der übrigen Welt hat, gebührt ihr nach historischen Vorbildern auch die führende Rolle."

The Year of the Grand Disillusion
Das Jahr der großen Enttäuschung

Die Vereidigung Henry Kissingers als Außenminister fällt in die letzten Monate einer Zeit, die er einst optimistisch als „das Jahr Europas" bezeichnet hatte. Kaum näher gekommen ist man den Zielen, die er für dieses Jahr gesetzt hatte: Neudefinierung und Wiederbestätigung der Prinzipien, die die atlantische Gemeinschaft gegenwärtig verbinden. Diese Stagnation hat teilweise ihre Ursache in der wachsenden Uneinigkeit Westeuropas. Die beispiellose Leichtigkeit, mit der sich der Warenaustausch unter den westeuropäischen Ländern abspielt, verhindert nicht, daß sich in der Europäischen Wirtschaftsgemeinschaft die größte Unzufriedenheit ihrer fünfzehnjährigen Geschichte ausbreitet.

In höchsten Maße alarmierend ist die ständige Verschlechterung der Beziehungen zwischen Paris und Bonn, die diesen Monat offen zutage trat, als der französische Landwirtschaftsminister und enge Vertraute Präsident Pompidous, Jacques Chirac, sich mit den Worten beklagte „ich bin bestürzt darüber, wie sich Deutschland von Europa abwendet". Bundeskanzler Brandt versuchte, die Äußerung abzuschwächen und stellte sie als Bemerkung eines kleinen Beamten hin. Einige Mitarbeiter des Kanzlers haben sich jedoch insgeheim revanchiert mit der Behauptung „die Franzosen leiden an mangelnder Logik. Sie schreien und protestieren wie kleine Kinder".

Derartige Streitereien verschlechtern die bereits gespannten Beziehungen zwischen Pompidou und Brandt. In Paris ist es ein offenes Geheimnis, daß Pompidou der Regierung Brandt mißtraut. Der französische Staatschef fürchtet, daß der stärker gewordene Einfluß der extremen Linken in Brandts Sozialdemokratischer Partei den Kanzler zu einem weniger zuverlässigen Partner in Sachen westeuropäischer Sicherheit machen könnte. Außerdem ist er der Meinung, daß die deutsche Regierung im Rahmen ihrer Ostpolitik mehr an einer Normalisierung ihrer Beziehungen zu den kommunistischen Ländern Osteuropas interessiert ist als an der Lösung der Probleme in Westeuropa. Ein Mitarbeiter Pompidous kommentiert: „Die EWG legt Deutschland Fesseln an. Wie würden die Deutschen reagieren, wenn die Sowjets ihnen in fünf Jahren die Wiedervereinigung anböten?" Die Franzosen beantworten sich die Frage selbst. Die Deutschen „würden ihre Akten einpacken und nach Bonn zurückkehren", aus dem Gemeinsamen Markt austreten und als Preis für die Rückgewinnung Ostdeutschlands „neutral" werden.

Lächerliche Befürchtungen. Brandts Mitarbeiter bezeichnen die französischen Befürchtungen als „lächerlich". Sie erklären, die westdeutsche Regierung habe keinerlei Absicht, neutral zu werden und weisen darauf hin, daß Westdeutschland es sich wirtschaftlich gar nicht leisten könnte, aus der EWG auszutreten. Der wahrhaft Schuldige, so behaupten sie, sei Paris, dessen Verschleierungstaktik und kleinliches Festhalten an Paragraphen und Vorschriften jeglichen Fortschritt in der EWG so lange verhindert haben. Genau so wie die Franzosen den Absichten Bonns mißtrauen sind die Westdeutschen davon überzeugt, daß die Franzosen wieder einmal einer Phase bedenklicher Handlungsunfähigkeit in ihrem eigenen Land entgegengehen. „Die Probleme der französischen Politik", so ein enger Berater Brandts, „resultieren aus einer innerfranzösischen Situation, in der sich für nichts, ob europäisch oder national, eine Mehrheit findet. Seit de Gaulle gibt es keine Stabilität mehr in Frankreich. Die französischen Politiker befinden sich politisch und wirtschaftlich auf einem Weg, von dem niemand weiß, wohin er führt."

Die Westdeutschen sind besonders verärgert, daß sich Frankreich einer Reform der Gemeinsamen Agrarpolitik (CAP) in der EWG widersetzt; aufgrund dieser Politik erhalten die französischen Bauern beträchtliche Subventionen, und die jährlichen Zahlungen Bonns an den Agrarfond betragen bereits mehr als eine Milliarde Dollar. „Das Ziel war eine Währungs- und Wirtschaftsunion bis spätestens 1980", erklärt ein westdeutscher Beamter. „Wo stehen wir heute, da uns nur noch sieben Jahre Zeit bleiben? Die Briten und die Deutschen bezahlen die französische Landwirtschaft. Das ist alles, aber es ist nicht genug." In der vergangenen Woche bemerkte Bundesaußenminister Walter Scheel: „Das Ziel (einer Union bis 1980) wird nie erreicht, wenn jede der interessierten Parteien sagt: ‚L'Europe c'est moi' (Europa bin ich)."

Vom Beitritt Großbritanniens zum Gemeinsamen Markt in diesem Jahr — zwölf Jahre lang von Frankreich verhindert — erhoffte man sich eine Wiederbelebung des Zweckdenkens, das einen deutsch-französischen Kompromiß ermöglichen könnte. Der holländische Ministerpräsident Joop den Uyl ist der Meinung, daß jetzt „Enttäuschung spürbar ist. All die alten Probleme sind in der erweiterten Gemeinschaft wieder aufgetreten." Aus diesem Grund bezweifeln viele Briten bereits die Richtigkeit ihrer lange debattierten Entscheidung „Europa beizutreten".

Die notwendig gewordene Einführung der 10 %igen Mehrwertsteuer auf alle Waren und Dienstleistungen hat den britischen Verbraucher, der zusätzlich mit einer 8,4 %igen Inflationsrate zu kämpfen hat, verärgert. Der Warenstrom vom Kontinent, zum Beispiel Kühlschränke aus Italien, Kraftfahrzeuge aus Frankreich, Lederwaren aus Deutschland, nach England fließt schneller als der Strom britischer Waren in die übrigen Mitgliedstaaten der EWG. Seit der Erweiterung des Gemeinsamen Marktes wurden in der EWG noch keine Programme, die für Großbritannien von direktem Nutzen wären, behandelt wie Investitionen in industriell nicht entwickelte Gebiete. So verwundert es nicht, daß nach der unlängst in Großbritannien durchgeführten Gallup-Umfrage 52 % der Befragten jetzt der Meinung sind, daß ihr Beitritt zum Gemeinsamen Markt ein Fehler war. Die in der britischen Öffentlichkeit weitverbreitete Unzufriedenheit mit der EWG wird London sicher zu einer unnachgiebigeren Haltung seinen Partnern im Gemeinsamen Markt gegenüber zwingen.

Dies alles ist kein gutes Omen für Kissingers Europapolitik. Er hatte gehofft, die Tagung der EWG-Außenminister am 10. und 11. September in Kopenhagen werde mit der Formulierung einer gemeinsamen Plattform enden, die einen einheitlichen europäischen Standpunkt zu den künftigen politischen und militärischen Aufgaben der Atlantischen Gemeinschaft darstellt. Die Chancen dafür stehen schlecht. Bestenfalls werden sich die Außenminister darüber einigen, wie und vor welchem Forum die EWG-Staaten Präsident Nixon bei seinem für diesen Herbst geplanten Europabesuch empfangen werden. Wenn diese kleinlichen Streitereien so weitergehen, — so die düsteren Prophezeiungen einiger Deutscher — wird Europa im Jahre 1980 nichts weiter sein als ein glorifizierter Supermarkt, gefüllt mit Waren aus den Ländern des Gemeinsamen Marktes.

More cultural contacts in Europe
Stärkere kulturelle Kontakte in Europa

Großbritannien hat die Absicht, während der nächsten vier Jahre zusätzlich 6 Mio. Pfund für ein Programm zum Ausbau seiner kulturellen Beziehungen zu anderen europäischen Ländern aufzuwenden. Das Programm wird sich nicht auf die traditionellen Gebiete des Kulturaustausches, wie Erziehung und Kunst, beschränken, sondern umfaßt auch den Jugendaustausch, den Austausch von jungen Arbeitern und unter Frauenverbänden sowie die Gründung von Partnerschaften zwischen Städten. Es ist geplant, neben dem bestehenden Konferenz-Zentrum in Wilton Park ein europäisches Diskussionszentrum zu gründen, und man hofft, ein britisches Kulturzentrum in Paris einzurichten. Erhöhte Aufmerksamkeit wird dem Sprachunterricht gewidmet.

Das Programm wurde am 6. März von Europa-Minister Geoffrey Rippon in einer schriftlichen Antwort im Unterhaus angekündigt. Die Initiative kommt zu einem Zeitpunkt, da Großbritannien sich in den letzten Phasen seiner Vorbereitung für die Mitgliedschaft in der erweiterten europäischen Gemeinschaft befindet und kann als Beweis für das neue „europäische" Denken angesehen werden, das jetzt vorherrscht. Obwohl die finanziellen Mittel in erster Linie für die Erweiterung der Beziehungen zu den Ländern der Gemeinschaft vorgesehen sind, betreffen einige Programmpunkte den Europarat, der noch andere Länder Westeuropas umfaßt.

Der vielleicht interessanteste Punkt des Programms sind die 50 Universitäts-Stipendien, die die Regierung alljährlich Universitätsabsolventen aus Westeuropa für ein Studium an britischen Universitäten anbieten will. Die Regierung hofft, daß andere europäische Länder diesem Beispiel folgen werden und ihrerseits britischen Universitätsabsolventen Stipendien an ihren Universitäten anbieten.

Von den 6 Mio. Pfund sind 3,5 Mio. dafür bestimmt, die Tätigkeit des British Council auszuweiten. Abgesehen von dem Stipendium-Projekt, wird der Council eine wesentliche Rolle bei der Verbreitung britischer Literatur spielen, ferner bei der Intensivierung der Zusammenarbeit zwischen europäischen Bibliotheken, der Schaffung von wissenschaftlichen und technologischen Informationszentren in bestimmten Ländern, der Verbesserung der Beziehungen zwischen Universitäten und der Förderung von Austausch und Begegnung zwischen Angehörigen der freien Berufe und Spezialisten.

Einen Teil der finanziellen Mittel für das neue Programm wird das Ministerium für Unterricht und Wissenschaft bereitstellen, um Lehrern aus anderen Ländern die Teilnahme an den vom Ministerium veranstalteten Kurzkursen für Lehrkräfte zu ermöglichen; um in Großbritannien ein europäisches Zentrum zu schaffen, das Informationen über derzeitige Forschungsarbeit auf dem Gebiet des modernen Sprachunterrichts liefert; um der Royal Society zu helfen, die Zahl der im Rahmen des westeuropäischen wissenschaftlichen Austauschprogramms vergebenen Stipendien zu verdoppeln und um den Austausch von jungen Arbeitern zu fördern.

European Road Construction

Der Straßenbau in Europa

Ausbau des Straßennetzes

In diesem Bericht wird der zunehmende Ausbau der Autobahnen und größeren Fernstraßen in den einzelnen Ländern Europas, vor allem in der EWG und der EFTA behandelt.

Ende des zweiten Weltkriegs verfügte nur Deutschland mit seinen mehr als 2000 km Autobahn über ein erwähnenswertes Autobahnnetz, das zwischen 1933 und 1942 entstanden war. 1953 hatten Italien und Holland mit dem Bau von Autobahnen begonnen. In diesem Jahr erreichten die Autobahnstrecken in Europa eine Gesamtlänge von 2 700 km. Von 1953 bis 1963 wurde das Autobahnnetz um mehr als 9 % jährlich auf eine Länge von ungefähr 6 600 km ausgebaut. Bis 1967 erhöhte sich diese Zahl auf mehr als 10 000 km, was einer jährlichen Zuwachsrate von 12 % entspricht. In diesem Jahr wies Westdeutschland das am weitesten entwickelte Autobahnnetz auf, gefolgt von Italien, Frankreich und Großbritannien. In Frankreich wuchs das Autobahnnetz am schnellsten; an zweiter Stelle folgte Großbritannien.

Mit Ausnahme des Autobahnbaus werden in ganz Europa kaum neue Straßen gebaut, da das Schwergewicht auf dem Autobahnbau und dem Bau von Umgehungsstraßen in verkehrsreichen Gebieten liegt.

Personenverkehr

Selbst wenn sich von 1967 bis 1980 die Länge der Autobahnen erwartungsgemäß verdreifacht, wird man damit der immer größer werdenden Zahl von Autos auf den Straßen nicht Herr. Der Bau neuer Straßen wird in erheblichem Umfang zu einer noch stärkeren Benutzung des Kraftwagens führen. Durch eine neue Autobahn erhöht sich schätzungsweise die Kilometerleistung im Normalverkehr um 20 %, im Touristenverkehr um 50 %. Eine erhebliche Steigerung der durchschnittlichen jährlichen Kilometerleistung im privaten Personenverkehr wird jedoch nicht erwartet. Wegen der zunehmenden

Verkehrsdichte auf den Straßen und der immer stärker werdenden Konkurrenz der Reiseunternehmen mit billigen Pauschalangeboten benutzen die Touristen lieber das Flugzeug als das Auto, um an ihre, von den traditionellen Reiseländern weiter entfernt liegenden, Reiseziele zu gelangen. Immer mehr Geschäftsreisende weichen auf das Flugzeug aus und benutzen am Bestimmungsort Mietwagen. Dies wiederum bedeutet eine starke Ausweitung des Marktes für Leihwagenunternehmen; ihr Marktanteil wird jährlich um mehr als 20 %, bis 1980 auf 2 Mrd. Dollar, steigen.

Das Straßenbauprogramm wird einerseits zu einem erhöhten Einsatz von Privatwagen auf Kurzstrecken und andererseits zu einer stärkeren Benutzung von Bussen führen, was sich bei Kurzreisen wiederum nachteilig auf Bahn und inländische Fluggesellschaften auswirken wird. Der Anteil des Bahn- und Flugverkehrs an längeren Fahrten und an Urlaubsreisen zu entfernteren Zielen wird jedoch zunehmen.

Frachtverkehr

In vielen europäischen Ländern hat sich ein Großteil des Frachtverkehrs von der Schiene und den Wasserwegen auf die Straße verlagert. Da man nicht davon ausgeht, daß die Autobahnen und Fernstraßen den erhöhten Verkehrsbedürfnissen in den 70er Jahren genügen, versuchen die meisten europäischen Länder, vor allem jene mit hoher Verkehrsdichte, die stärker belasteten Verkehrsmittel vom Frachtverkehr zu entlasten und diesen auf Schiene und Binnenwasserwege zurückzuverlagern. In Deutschland zum Beispiel unterliegt der Frachtverkehr auf der Straße Restriktionen durch hohe Steuern und durch Sperrung der Autobahnen für den Schwertransport an Wochenenden.

Die britische Regierung hat die Absicht, die Verlagerung des Ferntransports von den stark beanspruchten Straßen auf die Schiene zu erzwingen. Die Maßnahmen beider Regierungen sind noch nicht lange genug in Kraft, um eine Aussage über ihre Wirksamkeit zu machen. In zunehmendem Maße wird jedoch darauf hingewirkt, den Schwertransport von den Städten oder stadtähnlichen Gebieten fernzuhalten.

"Common transport policy"
Gemeinsame Verkehrspolitik

Vor einem Jahr lehnte es die Regierung in einer ihrer ersten schönen Aktionen zum Umweltschutz ab, eine Steigerung der Lastwagengewichte von 32 auf 44 t zuzulassen. Es sieht jetzt ganz so aus, als werde sie dies zurücknehmen müssen, weil die EWG ein Maximalgewicht von 42 t vorschlägt, und wenn Großbritannien der Gemeinschaft beitritt, muß es sich nach deren Bestimmungen richten.

Aus demselben Grund wird der dem Parlament z. Z. vorliegende Gesetzentwurf über Beschränkungen für kontinental-europäische Lastwagen, die nach Großbritannien kommen, wahrscheinlich nicht sehr lange gültig bleiben. Das könnte bei manchen, und insbesondere bei den Bewohnern Ostenglands, die ohnehin empört sind über die gewaltige Größe der durch ihre alten Marktstädte donnernden ausländischen Lastwagen, den Eindruck hervorrufen, als habe Großbritanniens EWG-Beitritt auf dem Verkehrssektor, zumindest was die Umwelt angeht, katastrophale Folgen. Dies braucht jedoch nicht der Fall zu sein; sehr viel hängt von dem Erfolg der gegenwärtig zwischen Großbritannien und den Sechs geführten Verhandlungen über verschiedene Aspekte der Verkehrspolitik ab.

Aspekte des Umweltschutzes sind überraschenderweise vielleicht die geringsten Sorgen. Die von der EWG vorgeschlagenen größenmäßigen Beschränkungen sind im allgemeinen nicht großzügiger als die in Großbritannien geltenden. — Im Falle der Lastwagen-Höhen sind sie sogar strenger, denn dafür gibt es in Großbritannien gegenwärtig keine Begrenzung. Es wird zwar eine Erhöhung der zulässigen Lastwagengewichte vorgeschlagen, aber es gibt keinerlei Beweis dafür, daß ein 44-Tonner schädigender für die Umwelt sein muß als ein 32-Tonner. Die eigentliche Diskussion sollte sich um die Achslast drehen und nicht um das zulässige Gesamtgewicht (denn nur dadurch werden die Straßen beschädigt) sowie um eine strengere und wirksamere Bekämpfung der tatsächlichen Ursachen der Belästigung — Lärm, Abgase usw. —, ungeachtet der Größe und des zulässigen Gesamtgewichts der betreffenden Lastwagen.

Es kann dann örtlichen Verkehrsbestimmungen, die beispielsweise in der Londoner Innenstadt und auch andernorts bereits bestehen, überlassen bleiben, dafür zu sorgen, daß Lastwagen verschiedener Größen auf geeignete Routen beschränkt werden. Was die Bekämpfung von Umweltschädigungen durch den Verkehr angeht, so wäre es unfair zu behaupten, die Staaten der EWG lägen hinter Großbritannien zurück, und der EWG-Beitritt würde deshalb für Großbritannien einen Rückschritt bedeuten. Tatsache ist, daß diese Frage bisher sowohl in Großbritannien als auch in der EWG vernachlässigt worden ist; diese Vernachlässigung ist jetzt jedoch erkannt worden, und Großbritannien hat bei der Sicherstellung angemessener europäischer Aktionen eine bedeutende Rolle zu spielen.

Die eigentliche Lücke zwischen Großbritannien und den Sechs besteht auf den Gebieten der Verkehrspolitik, der Wirtschaftlichkeit und der kommerziellen Regelung, und hier liegt eine echte Gefahr, daß Großbritannien Rückschritte machen muß, wenn es seinen Unterhändlern nicht gelingt, die EWG voranzutreiben. Mit dem Verkehrsgesetz von 1968 und anderen Maßnahmen besitzt Großbritannien eine Verkehrspolitik, die der der anderen europäischen Länder und sogar der ganzen Welt weit voraus ist. Sie verleiht sowohl dem Straßen- als auch dem Schienenverkehr eine kommerzielle Freiheit, die es sonst nirgendwo gibt, und schafft mit sozialorientierten Zuschüssen für Busse und Züge eine bessere Basis als andernorts für die Anerkennung und Maximierung (obwohl die Maschinerie noch keineswegs perfekt ist) der separaten sozialen und kommerziellen Vorzüge des Verkehrssystems.

In den Ländern der EWG leiden sowohl der Straßen- wie auch der Schienenverkehr unter einer Armee von Bürokraten und einer riesigen Menge von Bestimmungen mit dem Ziel, den Wettbewerb und die kommerzielle Freiheit einzuengen, und es ist undenkbar — auf jeden Fall wäre es äußerst kostspielig —, daß Großbritannien nach drei erfrischenden Jahren fruchtbarer Entwicklung zu einer solchen Welt zurückkehren könnte. Glücklicherweise gibt es in der EWG Menschen, die die Notwendigkeit erkennen, diese Fesseln abzuwerfen und auf eine dynamischere und fortschrittlichere Verkehrspolitik zuzusteuern. Ihnen dabei zu helfen, sollte einer der wichtigsten ersten Beiträge Großbritanniens zur Gemeinschaft sein.

Trouble again with monster lorries
Wieder Sorgen mit den Lkw-Kolossen

Es ist wieder einmal an der Zeit, sich Sorgen über die LKW-Kolosse zu machen. Am vergangenen Donnerstag verabschiedete das Unterhaus in der dritten und letzten Lesung die Regierungsvorlage, nach der Ungeheuer der Landstraße vom Kontinent bei der Ankunft inspiziert und zurückgeschickt werden können, wenn sie den britischen Vorschriften hinsichtlich Gewicht, Größe und Sicherheit nicht entsprechen. Für den kommenden Monat stehen auf der Tagesordnung des EWG-Ministerrats Vorschläge der Europäischen Kommission, die — falls sie verwirklicht werden — eben diese britischen Bestimmungen null und nichtig machen würden, wenn wir der Gemeinschaft beitreten.

Die Vorschläge für die Heraufsetzung von Größe und Gewicht, die der Gemeinschaft jetzt vorliegen, sind bereits Gegenstand hitziger Auseinandersetzungen zwischen den derzeitigen Mitgliedern. Die britische Regierung zeigt sich ziemlich standfest in ihrer Ablehnung der vorgeschlagenen Gewichtserhöhung — aber keineswegs standfest genug. Denn während noch vor ein oder zwei Monaten die zuständigen Minister sich lautstark dahingehend äußerten, daß der Beitritt zum Gemeinsamen Markt keineswegs eine Anhebung des britischen Gewichtslimits bedeuten werde, ist die Regierung jetzt zu dem Schluß gekommen, daß eine gewisse Steigerung des zulässigen Gesamtgewichts von LKWs unvermeidbar ist. Sie wendet sich jedoch entschieden gegen die Annahme sämtlicher Vorschläge der Kommission. Dabei hat sie Verbündete unter den Sechs, in erster Linie Deutschland, aber auch Holland, und es ist anzunehmen, daß auch die anderen Beitrittsländer auf derselben Seite stehen werden. Im Endeffekt wird über die Bestimmungen für schwere LKWs in einem Tauziehen zwischen diesen Ländern und Frankreich entschieden werden, das sich — wie stets — als hartnäckig und unnachgiebig in der Verteidigung dessen erweist, was es als sein nationales Interesse betrachtet.

Im Kern geht es mehr um das Gewicht als um die Größe. Die von der EWG vorgeschlagene Achslast von 11,5 t und das zulässige Gesamtgewicht von 42 t sind vollkommen unannehmbar für Großbritannien, wo das Gesamtgewicht auf 32 t und die Achslast auf 10 t begrenzt ist. Für Straßenschäden ist die Achslast maßgebend. In Holland, Deutschland und Italien liegt die Grenze ebenfalls bei 10 t, obwohl nur die beiden erstgenannten entschlossen zu sein scheinen, sie dort zu belassen.

Das gesamte britische Straßennetz so zu verstärken, daß es die von der Kommission vorgeschlagenen Gewichte tragen kann, würde 300 Mio. Pfund kosten, zuzüglich 10 Mio. Pfund jährlich für den Bau neuer Straßen, ganz abgesehen von den erschreckend hohen Kosten für den Umweltschutz. Anscheinend ist jedoch die britische Regierung bereit, eine gewisse Steigerung des Gesamtgewichts zu akzeptieren, solange es unter 40 t bleibt. Darüber hinaus hat die Regierung offenbar keine Einwände gegen eine Erhöhung der gegenwärtig in Großbritannien zulässigen Länge von 15 m auf 15,5 m, wobei sie sich auf den Standpunkt stellt, daß es auf einen halben Meter mehr bei Fahrzeugen dieser Größe nicht ankomme. Aber das ist falsch. Diese Fahrzeuge sind für eine zivilisierte Umwelt ohnehin schon viel zu groß.

Was immer geschieht, Großbritannien sollte solche LKW-Kolosse mit größerer Härte aus den Städten und von der Landstraße verbannen. Notwendig ist ein genau festgelegtes Netz für den schweren Güterverkehr auf der Grundlage der Autobahnen mit besonderen Zufahrtsstraßen und Garagen/Lagerhäusern, die die Arbeitsbasis für die schweren Lastwagen bilden könnten.

Und natürlich müßte entschlossen an den Ausbau unseres Eisenbahnsystems gegangen werden, das einer unserer besten, aber auch am stärksten unterbewerteten Aktivposten ist.

Clean-Air Buff
Großreinemachen der Luft

Die strengen amerikanischen Bestimmungen über Kohlenmonoxyd- und Kohlenwasserstoffemissionen, die für alle neuen Automodelle ab 1975 gelten sollen, bereiten den Automobilherstellern starke Kopfschmerzen. Für Milton Rosenthal, Jurist und Hauptgeschäftsführer der Engelhard Minerals & Chemicals Corp., könnte Washingtons Forderung nach sauberer Luft zu einer wahren Goldgrube werden. Engelhard produziert einen katalytischen Konverter — einen Stahlzylinder mit einer platinbehandelten Wabenstruktur — der einen Teil der Giftgase in unschädliche Substanzen umwandelt. Mit diesem Konverter, er kostet nich einmal 50 Dollar, können die Automobilhersteller mit großer Wahrscheinlichkeit den Forderungen der Umweltschutzorganisationen entsprechen.

Verschiedene Firmen versuchen, ähnliche Geräte zu entwickeln. Da die 75er Modelle bereits auf den Reißbrettern sind, müssen die Automobilhersteller allmählich ihre Zulieferer unter Vertrag bringen. Ford hat als erster mit Engelhard vor kurzem eine „feste Abmachung" über die Lieferung der Hälfte der für 1975 benötigten katalytischen Entgiftungsanlagen getroffen. Andere amerikanische Autofirmen werden wahrscheinlich bald folgen, und der 58jährige Rosenthal, der als sehr exakt und gründlich gilt, sieht sich nach weiteren Kunden auch im Ausland um. Seiner Meinung nach werden Japan und Kanada ebenfalls bald Emissionsbeschränkungen einführen.

Engelhard ist eine außergewöhnliche Firma. Sie wurde lange Zeit von dem dynamischen Charles Engelhard geleitet, der bei seinem Tod im letzten Jahr ein Milliarden-Dollar-Unternehmen hinterließ, das er durch weltweiten Handel mit Edelmetallen und deren Bearbeitung aufgebaut hatte. Engelhard hat intensive Geschäftsbeziehungen zu der Anglo-American Corp. of South Africa Ltd., welche mit 30 % bei Engelhard beteiligt ist und von Harry Oppenheimer, dem südafrikanischen Bergbaumagnaten, geleitet wird. Rosenthal würde jedes neue Geschäft begrüßen, denn im letzten Jahr fielen bei einem Umsatz von 1,5 Mrd. Dollar die Gewinne der Firma von 36 Mio. auf 28 Mio. Dollar.

"A fresh breeze from Stockholm"
Eine frische Brise aus Stockholm

Die Ziele für die Konferenz in Stockholm über die Umwelt des Menschen sind hoch gesteckt. Die Konferenz wird als ein Wendepunkt in der Geschichte bezeichnet. In ihrer Deklaration sollte sie einen neuen internationalen Verhaltenskodex mit neuen Konzeptionen von Souveränität schaffen, der besser auf eine Welt zugeschnitten wäre, die endlich als „nur die eine Erde" gesehen wird.

In der Praxis sehen die Dinge anders aus. Die Nationen verhalten sich weiterhin wie Nationen — schlecht. Die Deklaration enthält einige wichtige neue Grundsätze der Verantwortung gegenüber der Umwelt, sie bestätigt jedoch auch die alten Ansprüche auf nationale Souveränität und das Recht eines jeden Landes, seine natürlichen Ressourcen auszubeuten.

Es wäre dennoch falsch, würde man die Konferenz in Stockholm zu zynisch beurteilen. Es ist eine neue Stimmung aufgekommen, und es könnte sein, daß der damit in Gang gekommene Ideenaustausch zwischen Politikern und Wissenschaftlern auf lange Sicht wichtige Ergebnisse zeitigt. Es gibt heute in der Tat eine ganze Reihe führender Politiker in einer ganzen Reihe von Ländern, die Wachstums- und Entwicklungspolitik aus einer neuen Perspektive heraus betrachten. Die Konferenz hat aber auch deutlich gemacht, ein wie hohes Maß an Überzeugungskraft noch notwendig ist.

Stockholm hat sich als nützlich erwiesen, denn es hat gezeigt, daß die Umweltexperten, wenn 114 Nationen sich zusammengefunden haben, nicht den Bekehrten predigen. — Im Gegenteil: Frankreich und China halten nach wie vor an ihrem Recht fest, die Atmosphäre mit Nukleartests zu verseuchen; die lateinamerikanischen Länder wachen eifersüchtig über ihre Interessen bei der Ausbeutung der großen Flüsse und Wälder; Japan stellt die Interessen der Walfischfänger vor die weltweite Sorge um das Überleben des Wals, und China weist den Pessimismus der Malthusianer und Exponenten anderer Schwarzmalereien verächtlich zurück.

Deshalb scheiterte das einwöchige Bemühen um einen Konsensus für die Deklaration an der Tatsache, daß es keinen weltweiten Konsensus gibt. Die Deklaration ist daher ein Flickwerk von Konzessionen an gegensätzliche Interessen und gegensätzliche Ideen. Und dies ist natürlich ein getreues Spiegelbild des Zustandes der Welt.

Gibt man zu, daß wir im Rahmen einer Politik rivalisierenden nationalen Selbstinteresses operieren müssen, dann sind Fortschritte zu verzeichnen. Auf der Konferenz in Stockholm einigte man sich auf eine eindrucksvolle Liste internationaler Programme — beispielsweise für die globale Überwachung der Meere und der Atmosphäre, für Studien über die Ressourcen an Boden, Wald und Energie, für den Schutz des vielfältigen genetischen Erbes der Welt an Pflanzen und Lebewesen. Die internationale Gemeinschaft der Wissenschaftler ist jedenfalls wahrhaft international im Geist und weiß, worauf es ankommt.

Dies alles sind jedoch Empfehlungen für Maßnahmen seitens anderer, seitens Regierungen oder regionaler Gruppen oder Hilfsorganisationen der Vereinten Nationen oder weltweiter Konventionen. Deshalb muß ein Ton skeptischer Zurückhaltung angeschlagen werden. Die Konferenz in Stockholm konnte nichts weiter tun, als sich auf Formulierungen einigen. Wenn die Vollversammlung zustimmt, wird es bald einen koordinierenden und anspornenden Generalrat für Umweltprogramme geben. Doch der Weg zu aktivem Handeln muß erst durch die Labyrinthgänge der UNO-Bürokratie führen.

Ist dies die Art von Struktur, die schnell genug die Umweltprojekte in die Wege leiten wird, deren Dringlichkeit jedermann kennt? Nehmen wir einmal an, es entwickelt sich auf Grund der Verschmutzung der Meere eine Krisensituation. Würden die Bürokraten rechtzeitig handeln? Hätten sie überhaupt genug Geld, um zu handeln? Die Prozesse politischen Handelns können so leicht die besten Ideen zunichte machen.

Spaceship earth or mucky rivers?
Raumschiff Erde oder verdreckte Flüsse?

Eine der erfreulichsten Äußerungen 1971 war Peter Walkers wiederholte Erklärung, daß die oberste Priorität seines Ministeriums darin besteht, die Qualität der Umwelt zu verbessern. Es war mehr als nur eine nachdrückliche Bekräftigung des Offenkundigen, denn die Einrichtung des Ministeriums für Umweltfragen durch Zusammenlegung einer Anzahl von Ministerien, die mit Kommunalverwaltung, Planung, Wohnungsbau und Verkehrswesen befaßt waren, erschien seinerzeit als ein etwas krasser Fall von Effekthascherei.

Walker — dies sei zu seiner Ehre gesagt — beweist, daß er es mit dem Titel seines Ministeriums ernst meint. Seine Pläne zur Säuberung der Flüsse, die Ankündigung schwerer Geldstrafen und sogar von Gefängnishaft für Umweltverschmutzung, die strengeren Maßnahmen hinsichtlich Lärm und Größe von Straßenfahrzeugen sowie einige Entwicklungsprojekte betreffende Entscheidungen, beispielsweise über den Standort des 3. Londoner Flughafens — dies alles sind Symptome für eine begrüßenswerte neue Einstellung. Die Tatsache, daß sie jetzt ohne ernsthaften Protest akzeptiert werden, beweist, wie rasch sich die Dinge ändern. Seit Jahrtausenden nimmt die Menschheit die Umwelt als etwas Selbstverständliches hin. Die Erkenntnis dessen, was wir ihr antun, ist erst im letzten Jahrzehnt, ja vielleicht sogar erst in den letzten Jahren gekommen. Von jetzt an, so könnte man sagen, wird die Umwelt uns nicht mehr loslassen.

Ob die Politiker es nun fertigbringen, das aufzuholen, was getan werden muß, bleibt fraglich. Optimisten können auf den Erfolg der Gesetzgebung über die Reinhaltung der Luft hierzulande und auch auf die Verbesserung des Zustands einiger Flüsse verweisen, noch ehe Walkers Säuberungskampagne anläuft.

Nicht aller Fortschritt führt zwangsläufig zur Katastrophe, wie die Pessimisten es darstellen. Nichtsdestoweniger machen die Pessimisten das Rennen und verlagern das Argument von der Ebene der uns unmittelbar berührenden Verschmutzungsprobleme auf die so globalen

Belange wie die Erschöpfung der Metall- und Brennstoff-Vorräte innerhalb von ein oder zwei Generationen. Die statistischen Trends stärken ihnen den Rücken, und so gehen sie denn weiter und verurteilen die Vergötterung des Wachstums als die Wurzel allen Übels. Die Welt, so argumentieren sie, verfügt nicht über ausreichende Naturschätze, um für die künftige Weltbevölkerung Ende dieses Jahrhunderts im entferntesten den Wohlstand zu gewährleisten, den die Industrienationen heute genießen. Folglich wird den Politikern erklärt, sie müßten für Wachstum als Haupttriebfeder ihrer Wirtschaftssysteme irgendeine Alternative finden. Das ist zweifellos sehr viel verlangt angesichts der Tatsache, daß dreiviertel der Weltbevölkerung arm bzw. sehr arm sind.

Doch das Dilemma wird nicht von selbst verschwinden. Man wird ihm 1972 — wenn auch zunächst erst mit vorbereitenden und sondierenden Schritten — zu Leibe rücken müssen. Im Juni soll in Stockholm eine UN-Weltkonferenz über die Umwelt des Menschen stattfinden. Die Konferenz wird dann von größtem Nutzen sein, wenn sie sich möglichst strikt auf das Kurzfristige und das Praktische beschränkt.

Die praktische Bekämpfung der Verschmutzung darf nicht leichtfertig als lächerliche Pfuscherei abgetan werden, während das „Raumschiff Erde" untergeht. Dem Untergang zusehen, kann eine rein emotionale Befriedigung sein. Es gibt ermutigende Beweise dafür, daß schlimme Zustände behoben werden können: Flüsse — und auch Meere — vermögen sich zu regenerieren; eine hochentwickelte Landwirtschaft könnte weitaus mehr Menschen ernähren; die Tierwelt zeigt oft bemerkenswerte Zähigkeit und Anpassungsfähigkeit.

Die meisten Lösungen werden ebensosehr von Technologie und technischem know-how wie von politischen Entscheidungen abhängen. Es gibt kein Entrinnen in irgendein Utopia ohne Städte, ohne Autos, ohne Schulen. Das Problem heißt, eine auf den Naturwissenschaften gründende Industriezivilisation zu stabilisieren. Maßnahmen gegen die Verschmutzung werden zugegebenermaßen allein nicht ausreichen. Viel weiter gefaßten Grundsatzfragen wird man sich stellen müssen. Das freie Spiel wirtschaftlicher Raffgier auf dem freien Markt ist ein sicherer Weg ins Verderben, und wir werden einer neuen Werteskala bedürfen, die Quantität des Wachstums durch Qualität des Wachstums ersetzt. Aber das ist eher ein Thema für eine Generation statt für ein neues Jahr oder 10 Tage in Stockholm.

Take a sober look at doomsday
Der Katastrophe ins Auge sehen

Wenn 10 Tage in der Politik eine lange Zeit sind, so sind 10 Jahre praktisch unvorstellbar. Das mag sich als das Kernproblem dessen erweisen, was die Umweltspezialisten jetzt als das große Dilemma der Menschheit bezeichnen. Offensichtlich kann die Welt bei begrenzten Ressourcen kein unbegrenztes Wachstum aufrechterhalten; wie viele Politiker glauben jedoch, daß dies irgendetwas mit der Politik dieses oder des nächsten Jahres zu tun hat?

Der Club von Rom, eine internationale Gruppe von Naturwissenschaftlern, Wirtschaftlern, Industriellen, Beamten und prominenten Hochschulvertretern versucht z. Z. die Welt davon zu überzeugen, daß sie etwa innerhalb der nächsten 100 Jahre einer Katastrophe entgegengeht, wenn Bevölkerungszunahme und Wirtschaftswachstum im derzeitigen Umfang anhalten. Plötzlich — und zwar sehr bald — wird der Bedarf an Nahrungsmitteln und natürlichen Hilfsquellen dieser oder jener Art das Angebot übersteigen, und der Vorrat an einigen wichtigen, nicht erneuerungsfähigen Rohstoffen wie Erdöl und verschiedenen wichtigen Metallen wird erschöpft sein. Die Folge ist der wirtschaftliche und soziale Zusammenbruch.

Einige düstere Prophezeiungen sind als hysterisch kritisiert worden. Der Bericht des Clubs von Rom mit dem Titel „Grenzen des Wachstums" ist eine nüchterne, wenngleich deprimierende, technische Untersuchung der mutmaßlichen Trends in den nächsten 130 Jahren, die von einem Team von Computer-Experten am Massachusetts Institute of Technology durchgeführt wurde. Zweifellos werden sich einige der Mutmaßungen, die einem komplizierten Computer eingefüttert wurden, als falsch erweisen. Dennoch verlangt das MIT-Ergebnis eine sehr ernsthafte Prüfung. Vielleicht sind die Zahlenangaben falsch, aber der Beweis dafür muß erst erbracht werden. Vielleicht beurteilen die MIT-Experten die bisher unentdeckten Ressourcen oder das Potential der Sonnenenergie als Kraftquelle zu pessimistisch. Aber sie versuchten, unbegrenzte Hilfsquellen vorauszusetzen, und die Antwort, die sie bekamen, setzte lediglich den Beginn der Katastrophe zu einem späteren Zeitpunkt an.

Das Team gelangt im wesentlichen zu zwei Schlußfolgerungen: Zum einen, daß die Geburten- und die Sterberate einander angeglichen werden müssen, und zum andern, daß die Kapitalinvestitionen die Kapitalwertminderungen nicht überschreiten dürfen (die These vom Nullwachstum). Wachstum muß durch Stabilisierung ersetzt werden. Aber bei welchem Stand der Entwicklung? Und wann? Die Entwicklungsländer sind erst auf dem Weg zu dem Wohlstand, den andere begünstigtere Länder schon genießen.

Der Club von Rom ist sich in dem Streben nach einem Zustand globalen Gleichgewichts des moralischen und politischen Dilemmas bewußt. Wenn jedoch die Berechnungen in diesem Bericht auch nur annähernd stimmen, könnten die Kosten einer Verschleppung dieses Problems auf politischer Ebene für unsere Kinder und Kindeskinder erschreckend sein. Die Regierungen können nicht behaupten, sie seien nicht gewarnt worden. Die Warnung könnte sich als übertrieben erweisen, aber es wäre voreilig, sie ohne Beweis des Gegenteils als solche anzusehen.

World food situation worst for years

Schlechteste Weltnahrungsmittelsituation seit Jahren

Die Ernährungslage in der Welt ist in diesem Jahr schlechter als zu irgendeiner Zeit nach dem zweiten Weltkrieg, wenn man von den unmittelbaren Nachkriegsjahren absieht. 1973 wird wohl zum ersten Mal seit dem Krieg die Nahrungsmittelerzeugung der Welt tatsächlich zurückgehen, und das bei einer ständig wachsenden Bevölkerung.

Diese düstere Analyse wurde am Montag vom Generaldirektor der FAO in Rom, Dr. A. H. Boerma, veröffentlicht. Der Bericht wurde verfaßt, noch ehe die diesjährige Ernte eingebracht war, doch veranlassen die schlechten Ergebnisse des Jahres 1972 Dr. Boerma bereits, noch schlimmere Konsequenzen für dieses Jahr vorherzusagen.

Bei einem Zuwachs der Weltbevölkerung von 2 % fiel die Nahrungsmittelherstellung und landwirtschaftliche Produktion um 3 % pro Kopf und die Fangergebnisse der Fischerei um 1 %.

„Die Getreidevorräte sind auf den niedrigsten Stand seit 20 Jahren zurückgegangen", so Dr. Boerma. „In der neuen Situation weltweiter Verknappung schießen die Preise in die Höhe, und der Welt größter Exporteur landwirtschaftlicher Erzeugnisse mußte Exporteinschränkungen für bestimmte Produkte einführen (die amerikanischen Restriktionen für Sojabohnen).

In den Entwicklungsländern hat es zwei Jahre hintereinander Mißernten gegeben. 1972 konnte der Nahe Osten als einziges Entwicklungsgebiet eine große Steigerung verzeichnen, während der erhebliche Rückgang von 4 % im Fernen Osten einen Rückgang von etwa 1 % in der Gesamtnahrungsmittelerzeugung der Entwicklungsländer verursachte."

Dr. Boerma weist darauf hin, daß zwar 1971 eine sehr gute Ernte in den reichen Ländern erzielt wurde, im letzten Jahr jedoch der Rückgang in den Entwicklungsländern durch verheerendes Wetter in der Sowjetunion noch verschlimmert wurde, was zu Verknappung auch in den reichen Ländern führte.

Die Weltvorräte an Weizen sind, bedingt durch massive Käufe seitens der Sowjetunion, auf den niedrigsten Stand seit 20 Jahren gesunken, und die Reisvorräte gehen ebenfalls zur Neige.

„Für den Fall einer weitverbreiteten Mißernte im Jahre 1973 gibt es fast keine Reserven mehr, und die Welt hängt in erschreckendem Maße von der laufenden Produktion und damit vom Wetter ab."

Trotz einiger Schäden in der Sowjetunion hat die Ernte im allgemeinen die Erwartungen erfüllt. Dennoch warnt Dr. Boerma: „Der tiefere Grund für unsere Besorgnis ist, daß ein geringer Rückgang in einem größeren Gebiet 1973 zu einem ernsten Defizit in der gesamten Welt führen könnte, während eine leichte Verbesserung die bereits gefährliche Situation kaum erleichtern würde."

Während der Getreidehandel eine Aufstockung der Läger für das nächste Jahr vorausgesagt hat, ist Dr. Boerma der Meinung, daß es noch viel zu früh sei, eine zuverlässige Vorhersage über das Ergebnis zu machen, da zuviel vom Wetter abhänge. Außerdem hätten die Entwicklungsländer in diesem Jahr besondere Schwierigkeiten bei der Aussaat wegen der Verknappung und der hohen Preise für Kunstdünger auf dem Weltmarkt.

Two significant post-war years
Zwei bedeutsame Nachkriegsjahre

Das Internationale Institut für Strategische Studien zieht in seiner strategischen Untersuchung für das Jahr 1971 einen sorgfältigen Vergleich zwischen dem vergangenen Jahr und 1947, als historisch gesehen den vielleicht beiden wichtigsten Jahren seit dem Krieg. Der Nachwelt obliegt das Urteil, doch die einstweiligen Überlegungen sind interessant, da die Ähnlichkeit der beiden Jahre in ihrer Unähnlichkeit besteht. Aus beiden Jahren ging die Welt, nachdem sie wie ein Kaleidoskop durchgeschüttelt worden war, mit einem unverkennbar neuen Gesicht hervor. 1947 war es der kalte Krieg zwischen den Vereinigten Staaten und der Sowjetunion, der in plastischer Form zutage trat. 1971 erfuhr die alte Ordnung, zumindest in Asien, eine drastische Änderung, nachdem China und Japan — zwei Nationen mit nichtweißer Bevölkerung — deutlicher wahrnehmbar auf der Bühne erschienen.

Die Schwierigkeit, aus dem vergangenen Jahr große Schlüsse zu ziehen, liegt darin, daß so viel von dem, was in den 12 Monaten geschah, mehr der Zukunft denn der Vergangenheit angehört. Einige konkrete Ergebnisse sind zu verzeichnen, insbesondere der erfolgreiche Ausgang der Berlin-Gespräche, die längst fällige Aufnahme Chinas in die Vereinten Nationen, der Aufstieg Indiens zur vorherrschenden Macht auf dem Subkontinent durch einen Sieg über Pakistan in dem 14-Tage-Krieg vor Weihnachten und der Abzug britischer Truppen aus Singapur und dem Persischen Golf. Doch wesentlich mehr wurde in die Wege geleitet, ohne daß irgend etwas sehr Greifbares dabei herauskam.

Die Gespräche über eine strategische Rüstungsbegrenzung (SALT) versprachen eine gewisse Einigung zwischen Amerika und der Sowjetunion in diesem Jahr — eine Einigung, die sich auf Defensivwaffen konzentrieren dürfte unter Einbeziehung auch von Offensivwaffen. In Südostasien ging die Vietnamisierung weiter, und die Amerikaner zogen ihre Truppen stufenweise ab. Japan versetzte China einen sanften Rippenstoß in dem Versuch, in einem sich wandelnden Osten Freunde und Einfluß zu gewinnen.

Alles in allem gab es zweifellos mehr Wortgeschrei denn Kriegsgeschrei und erfreulicherweise konzentrierte es sich größtenteils auf Rüstungskontrolle oder verwandte Themen. Doch nicht alles Reden erbrachte das, was man sich vielleicht erhofft hatte. Wenn 1971 das Jahr war, in dem — wie das IISS es formuliert — ein „Großmächte-Viereck" in Ostasien und ein „neues Konzert von Großmächten" auf weltweiter Ebene entstand, was wird dann 1972 bringen? Der 1971 versprochene Vertrag über ein Verbot bakteriologischer Waffen ist Realität geworden. Doch Manlio Brosio, der als Abgesandter der NATO in Moskau Gespräche über ausgewogene Truppenreduzierungen führt, wartet noch immer hinter den Kulissen auf ein Stichwort von Breschnjew. Die politische Krise in der Bundesrepublik droht die Ostpolitik hinauszuzögern, und jedes Gefühl der Selbstgefälligkeit, das im Zusammenhang mit Vietnam je aufgekommen sein mag, hat sich als sehr unrealistisch erwiesen.

Als das konstanteste Element in diesem Jahr, im vergangenen Jahr und in den unmittelbar vorausgegangenen Jahren muß jedoch die wachsende Macht und Einflußnahme der Chinesen gelten — trotz ihres Rückschlags im indisch-pakistanischen Krieg, als sie auf Seiten des Verlierers standen und ihn nicht unterstützten. Die sowjetischen Truppenkonzentrationen in den militärischen Distrikten entlang der 11 200 km langen Grenze mit China machen diese Entwicklung deutlich.

Die Verdreifachung der Stärke dieser Truppen in den letzten drei Jahren zielt laut Studie eindeutig darauf ab, die Art bewaffneter Zwischenfälle „abzuschrecken oder unter Kontrolle zu haben", zu denen es 1969 im Gebiet des Ussuri-Flusses kam, und den Russen muß mehr an „Abschreckung" gelegen sein. Militärisch gesehen bleibt China in der Unterliga hinter den Supermächten zurück, da die Entwicklung einer Interkontinentalrakete von 6 400 km Reichweite vermutlich noch mehrere Jahre auf sich warten lassen wird.

Diplomatisch hingegen hat sich China durch eigene Energie oder vielmehr durch ein Auflockern seiner Haltung Einlaß in die Oberliga verschafft und ist in der östlichen Hemisphäre zu einer Kraft geworden, die die beiden Supermächte nie wieder werden ignorieren können. Dieser Aufstieg zusammen mit dem Japans war das eigentliche Charakteristikum des Jahres 1971. Vielleicht brachte nicht einmal 1947 etwas so Bedeutendes.

Agreement on Enough
Weitreichende Vereinbarung

In der vergangenen Woche kündigte das Weiße Haus an, es sei „ein wesentlicher Fortschritt" bei den seit 1969 laufenden Gesprächen über eine strategische Rüstungsbegrenzung (SALT) erzielt worden. Der Fortschritt — ein in einem geheimen Briefwechsel zwischen Präsident Nixon und dem sowjetischen Parteichef Leonid Breschnjew erzielter Kompromiß — stellt einen bedeutenden Meilenstein in den amerikanisch-sowjetischen Beziehungen dar und spiegelt eine Änderung auf lange Sicht in der Politik Washingtons wider. Wo einst die Vereinigten Staaten eine totale atomare Überlegenheit aufrechterhalten wollten, hat sich Washington jetzt zu dem entschlossen, was Nixon „Angemessenheit" nennt, das heißt ein Rüstungspotential, das jeden russischen Angriff durch die Möglichkeit eines vernichtenden Vergeltungsschlags vereitelt.

Obwohl noch viele schwierige Details von den derzeit in Helsinki tagenden SALT-Unterhändlern ausgearbeitet werden müssen, zeichnete sich silhouettenhaft eine Einigung der beiden Supermächte auf atomarem Gebiet ab. Die Vereinigten Staaten und die Sowjetunion haben sich auf eine Reihe von Begrenzungen und Einfrierungen geeinigt, wobei die Vereinigten Staaten einer Gleichstellung der Russen, und auf manchen Gebieten sogar einer zahlenmäßigen Überlegenheit, in jeder wichtigen Kategorie strategisch-atomarer Defensiv- und Offensivwaffen zugestimmt haben. Dafür haben die Russen ihrerseits zwei wesentliche Konzessionen gemacht. Sie stimmten einer zahlenmäßigen Begrenzung von raketenbewaffneten Unterseebooten zu. Viel wichtiger ist jedoch die Tatsache, daß sie sich bereit erklärten, von der jetzt vorgenommenen Einfrierung die taktischen Atomwaffen der Vereinigten Staaten in Europa und an Bord der Sechsten Flotte im Mittelmeer auszunehmen. Somit brauchten die Vereinigten Staaten ihre europäischen NATO-Verbündeten nicht zu beunruhigen, die argwöhnisch jedes einseitige Verhandeln mit den Sowjets über amerikanische Waffen, die zur Verteidigung Europas bestimmt sind, verfolgen würden.

Jedenfalls wurde durch den erzielten Kompromiß sichergestellt, daß Nixon, wenn er im Laufe des Monats Moskau besuchen wird, und Breschnjew die Zeremonie einer historischen Vertragsunterzeichnung werden erleben können. Wahrscheinlich werden sie zwei Dokumente unterzeichnen müssen. Zum einen einen bereits vereinbarten, ausgereiften Vertrag, der die Anzahl von ABM-Abwehrwaffen (oder Anti-Raketen-Raketen), die beide Seiten vielleicht installieren werden, begrenzt. Zum andern wird es, von Schwierigkeiten in allerletzter Minute einmal abgesehen, eine Vereinbarung zwischen den beiden Politikern geben, die informell die Anzahl strategischer Offensivraketen begrenzt, bis die SALT-Unterhändler einen offiziellen Vertrag vorweisen können. Die wesentlichen Punkte dieser beiden Dokumente sind:

ABMS: Die Vereinigten Staaten und die Sowjetunion dürfen jeweils nur zwei Anti-Raketen-Raketenanlagen mit jeweils einhundert Raketen unterhalten. Die Sowjets, die sich zur Verteidigung von Wohngebieten entschlossen haben, werden wahrscheinlich die Zahl ihrer 64 in einem Ring um Moskau aufgestellten Anti-Raketen-Raketen erhöhen. Sie werden vielleicht auch ihre Flugabwehrraketenstation Tallin in der Nähe von Leningrad in eine Anti-Raketen-Raketenstation verwandeln. Die Vereinigten Staaten, die sich im Gegensatz zur Sowjetunion entschlossen haben, die verstreut installierten Anti-Raketen Raketen zum Schutz ihrer auf dem Land stationierten Raketenstreitkräfte einzusetzen, hatten ursprünglich ihre Absicht kundgetan, 14 Safeguard-Raketenabwehrkomplexe zu errichten. Sie werden jetzt allerdings nur ihre beiden Anlagen in Grand Forks, North Dakota und Malmstrom, Mont., fertigstellen.

ICBM: Bis zur Unterzeichnung eines offiziellen Vertrages werden die beiden Supermächte die Anzahl ihrer Interkontinentalraketen auf dem derzeitigen Stand belassen, was für die Vereinigten Staaten eine Benachteiligung im Verhältnis von 2 zu 3 (1 054 zu 1 550) bedeutet. Beiden Seiten steht es frei, alte Raketen durch neue zu ersetzen. Viel wesentlicher ist allerdings die Tatsache, daß keine Begrenzung der atomaren Sprengkraft (in Megatonnen) zustande kam, ein Bereich, in dem die Sowjets die Vereinigten Staaten weit überrundet haben und es ihnen somit ermöglicht wird, den Nachteil ihrer weniger zielsicheren Raketen auszugleichen. Einige Experten im Pentagon rechnen in der Tat damit, daß die Russen in den großen leeren Silos, die kürzlich von amerikanischen Aufklärungssatelliten entdeckt wurden, neue Interkontinentalraketenkolosse installieren werden. Die Vereinigten Staaten haben mehr Sprengköpfe auf ihren Raketen — 5 700 im Verhältnis zu 2 500 bei den Russen — aber auch hier steht es Moskau nun frei, gleichzuziehen. Die Vereinigten Staaten haben zur Zeit einen beträchtlichen Vorsprung auf technologischem Gebiet. Ihre MIRV (Weltraumrakete mit Vielfachsprengkörper) können auf weit auseinander liegende Ziele gelenkt werden. Die russischen MRV (Weltraumraketen) treffen dagegen nur vorher fixierte Punkte.

Raketenbewaffnete U-Boote: Im Rahmen der vereinbarten zahlenmäßigen Begrenzung ist es den Sowjets, die bei der Entwicklung von Unterwasserraketen weit hinter den USA zurückliegen, erlaubt, die siebzehn im Bau befindlichen U-Boote fertigzustellen; innerhalb der nächsten Jahre werden die raketenbewaffneten U-Boot-Streitkräfte Moskaus ein U-Boot mehr besitzen als die 41-U-Boot-starke amerikanische Unterwasserraketen-Flotte.

Wenn auch bei dem für Offensivwaffen erzielten Kompromiß technische Verbesserungen erlaubt sind — die Vereinigten Staaten können zum Beispiel ihre raketenbewaffneten U-Boote durch ein Unterwasser-Langstrecken-Raketensystem (ULMS), wobei ein U-Boot ohne Waffen 165 Mio. Dollar kostet, ersetzen — so stellt er doch einen hoffnungsvollen Schritt auf dem Weg zur Einstellung des atomaren Rüstungswettlaufs dar. Er wird auch, so hofft man, als Richtlinie für einen ausgereiften Vertrag dienen, in dem eine Regelung für Offensivraketen vorgesehen ist, ähnlich wie auch die ABM unter Kontrolle gebracht wurden. Wenn es dazu kommt, wird der Vertrag über strategische Waffen historisch gleichbedeutend sein mit dem Atomtest-Stoppvertrag (1963) und dem Vertrag über atomare Lieferungsbegrenzung an dritte Länder (1968).

Quellenangabe

Consumer Income and Spending. The Conference Board: The U.S. Economy in 1990. New York 1972.
THE POOR Getting poorer and poorer. The Sunday Times, October 1973.
Growth Potential of the U.S. Economy. The Conference Board: The U.S. Economy in 1990. New York 1972.
Workers in the boardrooms. The Guardian Weekly, No. 14, March 1973.
See How They Grow. Time, May 1972.
The example of Shell International. The Financial Times, April 1972.
On with Exxon. Time, May 1972.
Facing the economic facts of life. The Guardian, February, 1973.
How to Fight Inflation. The Times, June 1972.
Bonn hopes to deflate the boom. The Guardian, February, 1973.
A Secret IMF Proposal for Monetary Reform Urges Radical Changes. The Wall Street Journal, May, 1972.
What Marshall Aid did for Europe. The Times, June 1972.
The Year of the Grand Disillusion. Time, September 1973.
More cultural contacts in Europe. Engl. Rundschau, Juni 1972.
European Road Construction. Stanford Research Institute: A Summary of Report No. 390, December 1969.
Common transport policy. The Times, December 1971.
Trouble again with monster lorries. The Sunday Times, April 1972.
Clean-Air Buff. Time, May 1972.
A fresh breeze from Stockholm. The Guardian, June 1972.
Spaceship earth or mucky rivers? The Guardian, January 1972.
Take a sober look at doomsday. The Guardian, March 1972.
World food situation worst for years. The Guardian, September 1973.
Two significant post-war years. The Times, May 1972.
Agreement on Enough. Time, May 1972.

Public Relations

Von Dr. H. L. Zankl

In 300 Leitsätzen mit eingehenden Erläuterungen wird der Gesamtbereich der Public Relations dargestellt. Die wissenschaftlich fundierten Ausführungen sind sehr praxisnah geschrieben. Ausgehend von den Grundbegriffen und dem Wesen der Public Relations, behandelt der Autor nach einem Exkurs über öffentliche Meinung die Funktionen der Public Relations, die Organisation, den Ablauf einer Aktion und das Instrumentarium. — Das Buch ist nicht nur für Fachleute bestimmt, sondern vor allem auch für Nachwuchskräfte und für Studierende aller Fachrichtungen. 160 Seiten, br. 24,80 DM

Die programmierte Prüfung des Großhandelskaufmanns

Von E. Hüttner / H. Klink

Die hier zusammengestellten Aufgaben aus den Gebieten Betriebskunde, Rechnen und Buchführung entsprechen in Art und Schwierigkeit den Abschlußprüfungen. Sie wurden und werden in ähnlicher Form tatsächlich gestellt.

Zu jeder Frage werden mehrere Antworten vorgegeben; welche davon richtig sind, wird jeweils auf der folgenden Seite angegeben. Im Rechenteil ist dort auch der Lösungsweg in knapper, aber einprägsamer Form dargestellt. Der Prüfungskandidat sollte zunächst selbst den Versuch unternehmen, die zutreffenden Antworten zu finden. Erst danach sollte festgestellt werden, welche von den vorgegebenen Antworten richtig sind. 364 Seiten, br. 28,50 DM

Der Brief des Kaufmanns

Lehr- und Übungsbuch für den kaufmännischen Schriftverkehr

Von Dr. P. Feldkeller

Dieses Buch zeigt, wie der Brief im Wirtschaftsleben logisch richtig aufgebaut, psychologisch klug abgefaßt und stilistisch einwandfrei formuliert wird, damit er den gewünschten Erfolg bringt. Unter diesen Gesichtspunkten behandelt Feldkeller alle in einem Unternehmen vorkommenden Geschäftsvorfälle an Hand von klaren Erläuterungen, Briefbeispielen und vielen Übungen mit Lösungen. Jede Situation ist anders, erfordert „maßgeschneiderte" Briefe (das gilt auch für die Textprogrammierung!). Der Leser jedoch, der Feldkellers Buch studiert, wird in jeder Lage den richtigen Brief schreiben können. 14. Aufl., 280 Seiten, br. 24,80 DM

Mathematik — Grundkenntnisse für Betriebswirte

Von Prof. J. Sommerfeld

Um auch dem mathematisch weniger vorgebildeten Leser die Möglichkeit zur Erarbeitung dieses Stoffgebietes zu geben, beginnt dieser Beitrag mit den Grundrechenoperationen. Darauf aufbauend werden die Prozentrechnung und ihre Umkehrung, die Mengenlehre, die elementaren Funktionen und Bestimmungsgleichungen behandelt. In dem Abschnitt „Analysis" geht es um Folgen, Reihen und die Finanzmathematik, ferner um die Differential- und Integralrechnung. 224 Seiten, br. 23,80 DM

Betriebswirtschaftlicher Verlag Dr. Th. Gabler, Wiesbaden, Postfach 11

Handbuch des Kaufmanns

Hrsg.: Dr. J. G r e i f z u

unter Mitwirkung führender Fachleute aus Wirtschaft und Wissenschaft

Das Handbuch enthält alles, was der Kaufmann bei der täglichen Arbeit wissen muß und brauchen kann. Vom Rechnen und Buchführen bis zur Planung und Organisation, von wichtigen Formularen und Statistiken bis zur Praxis der Betriebe und Volkswirtschaft. Die systematische, übersichtliche Gliederung läßt die großen Zusammenhänge klar hervortreten. Jedes einzelne Sachgebiet ist prägnant und doch erschöpfend dargestellt. Über 800 Beispiele, Muster, Tabellen usw. sowie zahlreiche Bilder auf Kunstdrucktafeln machen den Stoff anschaulich und erleichtern die praktische Auswertung. 18. Aufl., 1204 Seiten, Ln. 78,— DM

Brieflexikon für Kaufleute

In diesem Buch sind etwa 200 Musterbriefe in systematischer Anordnung zusammengestellt und erläutert. Jeder Vorgang in einer Unternehmung, ob es sich um den Wareneinkauf oder Warenverkauf, das Mahnwesen, die Firmengründung, die Kunden- oder Personalkorrespondenz oder um den Schriftverkehr mit Behörden, Bahn, Post handelt, wird erfaßt. Ein besonderer Abschnitt ist dem Schriftverkehr mit dem Finanzamt gewidmet. Neben dem Brieftext sind am Rande in Rotdruck Bemerkungen im Telegrammstil angebracht, die den Briefschreiber über die Besonderheiten bei Abfassung des betreffenden Brieftextes informieren. Ferner werden am Fuße jeder Seite kurzgefaßte Erläuterungen zur Sache und Hinweise auf Gesetze usw. gegeben. 5. Aufl., 244 Seiten, DIN A 4, Ln. 48,60 DM

Handbuch der Werbung

Mit programmiertem Fragenanhang und praktischen Beispielen von Werbefeldzügen

Hrsg.: Prof. Dr. K. Chr. B e h r e n s unter Mitwirkung führender Fachleute

In diesem Buch sind in 82 Beiträgen alle mit der Werbung zusammenhängenden Themenkreise behandelt und die zur Verfügung stehenden Lösungsmöglichkeiten fachgerecht erörtert worden.

Es ist vor allem für den Praktiker, also für die Auftraggeber und Durchführenden der Werbung sowie für Studierende der Werbewissenschaft gedacht. Auf über hundert Seiten wird die Planung, Durchführung und Kontrolle tatsächlich erfolgter umfangreicher Werbemaßnahmen in den verschiedenen Wirtschaftszweigen dargestellt.

Das systematische Inhaltsverzeichnis und vor allen Dingen zum Schluß das ausführliche Stichwortregister geben auf jede Frage sofort eine Auskunft. Mit den an mehreren Stellen des Werkes eingefügten **programmierten Fragen** mit Antworthinweisen, die der Selbstkontrolle des Lesers dienen sollen, wurde ein umfassendes **Lehr- und Studienbuch** geschaffen. 1180 Seiten, Hld. 184,80 DM

Betriebswirtschaftlicher Verlag Dr. Th. Gabler, Wiesbaden, Postfach 11